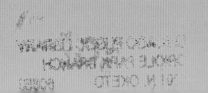

DIETRICH WILDUNG

SERIES EDITOR: HENRI STIERLIN
PHOTOGRAPHS: ANNE AND HENRI STIERLIN

EGYPT

From Prehistory
to the Romans

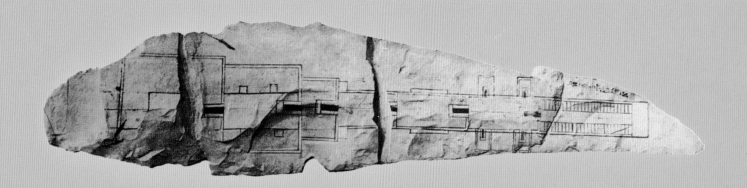

TASCHEN

KÖLN LISBOA LONDON NEW YORK PARIS TOKYO

Page 3
This plan of the tomb of Ramesses
IX, drawn on a large limestone
ostracon, was found in his tomb in
the Valley of the Kings. It is not a
draft plan, but a building record
after the completion of the tomb.
The notes name the rooms and
specify their sizes.
New Kingdom, Dynasty XX,
c. 1100 B.C.; Cairo, Egyptian
Museum

Page 5
This small papyrus capital belongs
to the group of architectural
models which preserve the old
building forms into the Ptolemaic Period and must have
been handed down as examples
of the traditional style.
Ptolemaic Period, third–first
century B.C.; limestone; Berlin,
Ägyptisches Museum

This book was printed on 100 % chlorine-free bleached
paper in accordance with the TCF-standard.

© 1997 Benedikt Taschen Verlag GmbH
Hohenzollernring 53, D-50672 Köln

Editor-in-chief: Angelika Taschen, Cologne
Edited by Susanne Klinkhamels, Cologne
Co-edited by Caroline Keller, Cologne
Design and layout: Marion Hauff, Milan
Cover design: Marion Hauff, Milan; Angelika Taschen, Cologne
English translation: Ingrid Taylor, Munich

Printed in Italy
ISBN 3-8228-8252-6

Contents

INTRODUCTION

Basic Architectural Forms in Ancient Egypt

Model of a cowshed
Lightweight structures made of wood and mats were typical of everyday architecture in Ancient Egypt. Designed to provide shade for a herd of cows, the roof of the shelter rests on lightweight supports made out of bundles of plant stems.
Early Middle Kingdom, Dynasty XI, c. 2000 B.C.; wood, stuccoed and painted; Munich, Staatliche Sammlung Ägyptischer Kunst

The image we have today of Ancient Egypt is beset with clichés: sinister mummies and the beautiful Queen Nefertiti, the death-bringing curse of the pharaohs and treasures shrouded in mystery distort our view of the achievements of the civilisation and culture of Ancient Egypt. It is a land which in ancient times formed the bridge between north and south, between Africa and the Mediterranean, and which, together with the Near East, is a cornerstone in the history of Western civilisation.

Just as the mummy can in no way be regarded as the leitmotif of religion in Ancient Egypt, nor can Nefertiti alone convey the essence of the art of the pharaohs, being instead merely an exception, mistakenly perceived as representative. She shares her fate as an inappropriate figurehead, a false symbol, with the pyramid, which is seen as the epitome of Ancient Egyptian architecture. Its clear, formal structure is generally perceived not only as the classic example of the art of Ancient Egypt, but also as the model for the political and social system of the pharaohs' empire.

This view conveniently takes the exceptional case of a purely geometric basic form and turns it into a standard, thus disregarding the continuous development of Ancient Egyptian architecture over a period of three thousand years. Egyptian architecture is a mirror of creation, a means of artistic expression that is firmly rooted in the realms of sensory perception. It is not a construct of mathematics, technology and abstraction. Often labelled as "monumental", this architecture, seemingly presented solely in terms of sacred buildings, in temples and tombs, has its actual origins in secular buildings, in the everyday architecture of an agricultural people – a fact which it never denied or sought to conceal.

The architecture of the pharaohs, as we perceive it today, is dominated by stone buildings, giving us the impression that stone was the main building material at the time. This impression of Ancient Egypt has arisen only as a result of our perspective looking back over thousands of years. The majority of buildings on the Nile actually consisted of easily degradable material, and even today, away from the big cities with their preference for concrete and fired brick, mud-brick construction still typifies many towns and villages. The silt deposits of the river Nile provide the most important building material. Unfired, air-dried bricks, loosened with chaff or sand, are not only easily obtainable and cheap, but, in the dry heat of the Nile valley, they play an important role in basic air conditioning inside the buildings. Indeed mud-brick architecture has enjoyed a revival worldwide in the last ten years, and it is not by chance that a key figure in this area is an Egyptian architect, Fathi Hassan, thus continuing a tradition that dates back to the fourth millennium B.C.

But very little of this ancient secular architecture of mud bricks, wood and reed mats has been preserved, whereas the stone temples and tombs have survived the millennia in some cases almost undamaged. The reason lies not only in the choice of building materials, but also in the sites selected for their construction, a decision influenced by considerations of function. Tombs and temples were generally built

Nile landscape in Lower Nubia
The most important raw material in secular architecture came from Egypt's main artery, the Nile. This river transports mud over thousands of kilometres from East Africa, through Nubia, and deposits it in the Nile valley in Egypt during the annual floods. This mud is used to make sun-baked bricks.

away from the valley floor, on the edge of the desert, above the water table and out of reach of the annual Nile floods. Everyday architecture – huts, houses, stables, workshops, etc. – was located on either side of the Nile, on the humid valley floor. These structures were subject to damp and intense use, so that after a few decades it became necessary to replace the old, dilapidated buildings with new ones – of not too expensive an undertaking in view of the ease of obtaining building material. Over the centuries and millennia, this rapid cycle of old buildings collapsing and new ones taking their place raised the level of the villages and towns to form small hills, known as *tells* in Arabic. Today these hills mark the site of ancient settlements, and often modern towns are to be found sitting on top of a pile of "rubble". Such sites present real problems for archaeological excavation. Walls of mud brick are very difficult to pick out in the silt of the Nile valley, and in many cases the ancient settlement lies below the groundwater level; excavation of these sites is only possible with a great deal of technical and financial input, and for this reason stratigraphical excavations which are so useful in investigating settlement history cannot be carried out.

Nevertheless it is possible to draw up a detailed picture of Ancient Egyptian secular architecture. Ancient architectural models, in particular from the early years of the Middle Kingdom (around 2040–1991 B.C.) show in small scale (about 1:25 to 1:40) the whole formal and functional range of buildings. Such three-dimensional models of wood or pottery were placed as grave objects in tombs during the early years of the Middle Kingdom, thus taking over the same function as that of the reliefs and paintings in the tombs of the Old Kingdom, i.e. preserving elements of life this side of the grave for the life in the hereafter. Despite an inevitable exaggera-

The mountains of West Thebes
Not far from the valley are the limestone mountains of Central and Upper Egypt which supplied the raw material needed to build the nearby temples and tombs. The quarries themselves became building sites, when underground tombs were excavated in them.

tion and idealisation of reality, these models are very realistic and represent a rich source of information; they can be compared with the types of building which can be seen to this day in the Nile Valley and in Central and West Africa.

Village architecture included simple shelters raised on stilts to provide shade underneath, kraal-like walled courtyards and flat-roofed buildings, often with steps leading up the outside to the roof. Daily life in larger settlements is revealed in the grain stores with domed and barrel-vaulted roofs, as well as workshops with several rooms for carpenters, weavers, butchers and bakers. Town housing is shown in models of houses with walled interior courtyards containing a pond surrounded with sycamores.

Architectural models made of limestone have survived from the first millennium B.C.; they show tower-like houses with several storeys, very similar to the type found nowadays in traditional urban architecture in the Yemen.

The particular significance of secular architecture in Ancient Egypt lies in the fact that the forms and materials used in this area can be traced also in the elements and structure of sacred architecture. Without a knowledge of the typical forms of architecture in mud bricks, wood and rush mats, it is difficult to understand the characteristic appearance of stone architecture.

The pylon, for example, a typical entrance structure in Egyptian temples since the New Kingdom, has walls that are not vertical, but instead slope outwards towards the bottom – a typical feature of mud-brick architecture, where the laws of statics dictate this form. Likewise, the rush bundles used in mud-brick buildings to reinforce edges, are reflected in stone architecture in characteristic three-quarter roll moulding. Finally at the top of the pylon is an "Egyptian gorge", consisting of a

cavetto and horizontal roll moulding, a form derived from a wreath of palm leaves, such as is still commonly found on the top of mud-brick walls in Egypt even today. This type of cornice has incidentally enjoyed renewed popularity as recently as the twentieth century, in postmodern architecture.

The time and effort involved in reproducing these architectural forms in stone is considerably greater and technically it is a more complex task than building in right angles with vertical walls. Egyptian architecture in stone produced forms that are not ideally suited to the building material of stone. Achieving an appropriate relation between building material and form was not a basic principle of Ancient Egyptian architecture.

An explanation of this is to be found not primarily in form but in iconography. The architectural form is not the goal, but the expression of a content. A temple with sloping walls is representative of a house, a house of the gods. The specifically sacred aspect is its permanent material, stone. Its formal elements, however, are taken from secular architecture; they are adaptations of motifs found in everyday buildings. Even in the very earliest stone architecture, in the funerary complex of King Djoser (around 2650 B.C.) the prototype columnar forms, which later became such a characteristic feature, can be traced back to models found in nature. The papyrus column with its tulip-shaped capital is seen here as an engaged three-quarter column; both in its longitudinal section and in its wedge-shaped cross-section it traces the shape of a stylised papyrus stem, with an umbel opening out at the top. As a load-bearing element intended to support the ton weight of the architrave and temple roof, a plant-shape would seem rather unsuitable. For the Egyptian builder, however, the content expressed by this form was the key issue, and his job was to

Valley plain near Memphis
In the damp Nile valley mud bricks used in building are subject to rapid decay. As a result the majority of Ancient Egyptian everyday architecture has now disintegrated and cannot be accessed by archaeological investigation. Much of the area which was once the capital city of Memphis is today just a flat expanse.

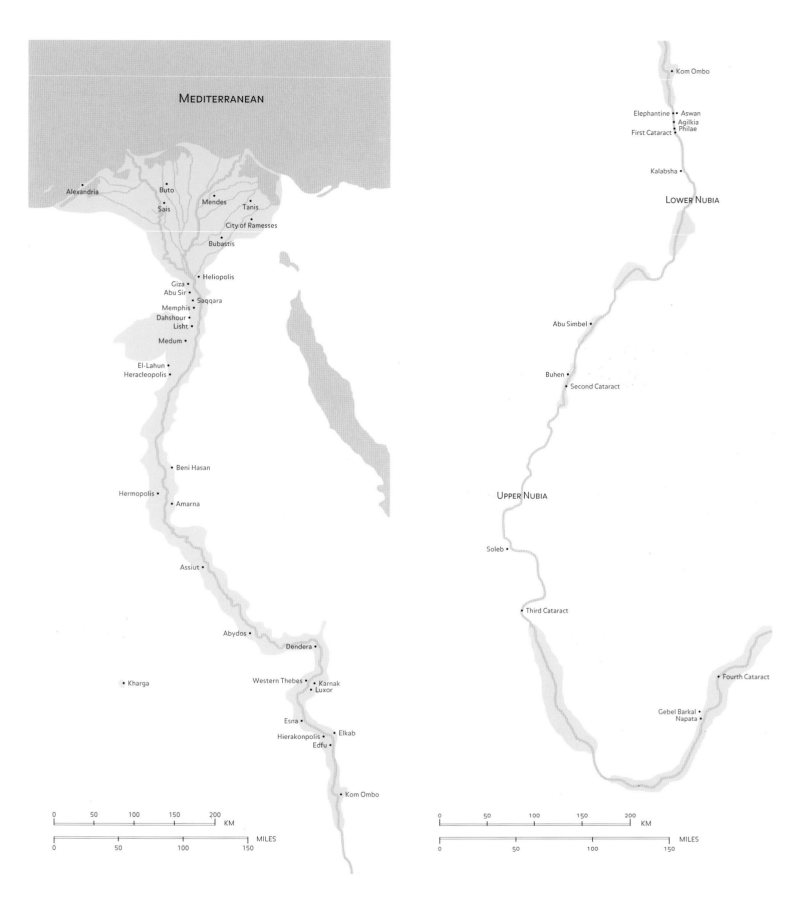

Map of Ancient Egypt

The geographical structure of the Egyptian Nile valley is unique. The Nile valley extends about 1 000 km north-south and to the south of Cairo it is just a few kilometres wide, in some places just a few hundred metres.

Model of a house
Although the mud-brick houses in
the villages and towns have long
since disintegrated, they are not
entirely lost to our view. Models
made of burnt clay bricks were
placed in tombs and they now
show us what these structures
looked like and how they were
built.
Early Middle Kingdom,
Dynasty XI, c. 2000 B.C.; burnt
clay bricks; Cairo, Egyptian
Museum

Page 13
House in Sanaa, Yemen
The closest equivalent today
of everyday Ancient Egyptian
architecture can be seen in the
mud-brick houses in the Yemen.
Details such as roll moulding to
strengthen corners and layers of
brick rising slightly at the corners
correspond to those found in Ancient Egypt.

find a technical solution to convey this. In Djoser's step-pyramid complex it is easy
to spot the natural forms which the builders used as their models. The half-columns
on the shrines of the ceremonial court and on the façades of the North and South
Buildings may at first be reminiscent of the fluting on Greek columns, but are in fact
quite clearly the monumental representation of plant stems, such as were commonly used as supports for lightweight tent-like structures.

In the temple architecture of Dynasty V the palmiform column is the dominant
column form. Its smooth, round shaft tapers slightly towards the top where horizontal banding ties in the carved palm branches that fan out vertically in fine pan-
icles. Still today in Egypt it is a common practice to bind palm-tree trunks at the bottom of the leaves, to encourage growth. When looking at the towering trunks of an
Egyptian palm grove, it is not hard to imagine where the Ancient Egyptian builders
drew inspiration for the idea of a column supporting a temple roof in the form of a
stone slab decorated on the underside with stars, to look like the heavens. The palm
column is nature turned into stone, it is the tree over which vaults the sky.

A fundamental and significant principle governing this transferral of secular
building forms and everyday building materials into stone architecture, and one
that held true for all Ancient Egyptian architecture, is that all forms are carriers of
meaning, they are legible, translatable concepts in a language of forms and have a
grammar which can be deciphered, taught and learned.

In the tombs of the Old Kingdom, from about 2400 B.C. onwards, there was an
exceptionally slender columnar form with the shaft in the form of a bundle of plant
stems. At the top the stems end in closed lotus blossoms, and small lotus buds are
placed between the stems. Clearly lotus stems are too unstable and lotus blossoms
too tender and fragile to support even the lightest tent roof, but the motif of the lotus has iconographic significance; it is the blossom that opens itself to the sun and
which, in the form of a column, gives the ceiling its function as the bright, sunlit sky.

The plant-like form of Ancient Egyptian columns is nowhere so evident as in the
court of Amenhotep III in the Temple of Luxor. Here it is the real sky that is held aloft
by the papyrus-bundle columns. In transferring the plant form to stone an inner so-
lidity is achieved as well as integrity as a supporting element; however its limits
seem to be reached in the Ramesside papyrus columns in the central axes of the Hypostyle Hall of the Temple of Amun in Karnak, in the Ramesseum from Western

Tall house in Sanaa, Yemen
These tower-like brick buildings, several storeys high, found in the Yemen, are one of the most remarkable achievements of secular architecture in the Near East.

Model of a tall house in Ancient Egypt
In Ancient Egypt, too, there were examples of houses several storeys high. Evidence of this is found in tomb paintings and in architectural models. Construction details can be identified particularly well in this model.
Late Period, first millennium B.C.; limestone; Cairo, Egyptian Museum

Roll moulding and cavetto

Great attention and effort was paid to the sculptural form of building corners and the tops of walls. The roll moulding to strengthen corners is derived from bundles of plants, and the cavetto, as its decoration shows, derives from palm leaves. Both motifs are stone versions of forms typically used in mud-brick architecture.

Pronaos of the Temple of Hathor in Dendera; Roman Period, first-second millennium B.C.

Roll moulding and temple wall

The roll moulding finishes off the edge of the temple wall and gives formal definition to the structure. The pictorial programme depicting the interaction between man and god is enacted on the wall, within the architectural framework of a house turned into a temple.

West side of the pylon of the Temple of Horus in Edfu; Ptolemaic Period, third–first millennium B.C.

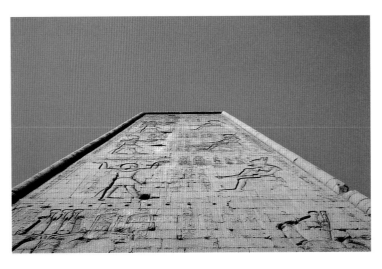

Thebes and in the Temple of Sethos in Abydos, where the papyrus buds in the capitals seem to open so wide that their edges fold outwards as if pressed down under the weight of the architrave and roof above. In their iconographic richness and stylistic balance the floral capitals of the Egyptian temples in the Ptolemaic-Roman period are a pinnacle of achievement in the evolution of plant columns in Egyptian architecture. Also to be noted, in addition to the composite capitals made up of several layers of papyrus buds of increasing size, are the floral capitals of the Temple of Khnum in Esna and of the Temple of Horus in Edfu which have grapes and different types of flowers interwoven into the column. They led on directly to the basket capitals of Egyptian architecture in the late classical period, and are at least indirectly one of the precursors of early Christian art in the West.

Enclosing wall of the Temple of Hathor in Dendera
The wall encircling the temple complex is of unbaked brick laid down in alternating convex and concave layers. The reason for this is primarily to do with stability, but it also has religious significance: it represents the waves of the primeval ocean, out of which the temple rises as a primeval hill. Roman Period, first–second millennium B.C.

Painted ceiling in a tomb
Evidence can be found for the decoration in Ancient Egyptian houses from the paintings found in tombs. As quasi-apartments for the deceased, these tombs had painted wall decoration in the form of carpets and mats such as would have been found in the houses at the time. Mats were also spanned across beams (here painted brown) to form roof constructions.
Western Thebes; New Kingdom, Dynasty XVIII, c. 1450 B.C.

Façade of a tomb in Beni Hasan
The tops of round beams rise out of the wall above the architrave. They are the representation in stone of a wooden frame on which rested the rushwork roof. Here on the façade of a rock tomb this form has no practical function, but it does have religious significance in that it turns the tomb into a house for the deceased.
Tomb of Khnumhotep; Middle Kingdom, Dynasty XII, c. 1850 B.C.

Papyrus columns in Saqqara
The prototype for the most popular columnar form in Ancient Egypt stands in the precinct of the Step Pyramid of Djoser in Saqqara. The papyrus stem and umbel are closely represented in a naturalistic fashion in the stone column and yet the overall shape is still a distinctive interpretation.
North house; Dynasty III,
c. 2600 B.C.; limestone

Plant column in Saqqara
The fluted half-columns on one of the cult buildings of the Step Pyramid complex in Saqqara are modelled on the shape of a plant stem.
South house; Dynasty III,
c. 2600 B.C.; limestone

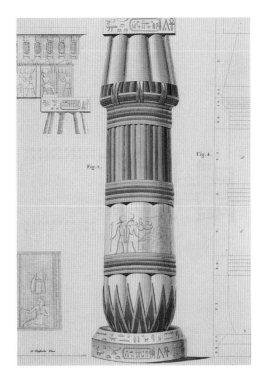

Clustered column
Often, only traces of the original
colouring of the columns have survived. This reconstruction shows
how the painted decoration helps
to envisage the architectural form
as nature represented in stone.
From: H. v. Minutoli, *Reise zur Oase
des Jupiter Ammon,* 1824

**Clustered columns in the Temple
of Luxor**
The basic motif in this columnar
form popular in the New Kingdom
is a bundle of papyrus stems with
closed umbels. As stone representations the delicate leaf tips
have the strength to support the
beams.
New Kingdom, Dynasty XVIII,
c. 1380 B.C.; sandstone

Plant capital
In the temples of the Ptolemaic Period the basic forms of Egyptian columns, which had been virtually unchanged over 2500 years, emerged in a wide variety of different shapes. Various plant motifs were combined to create veritable bouquets of flowers emerging from the surface of the stone.
Birth house of the Temple of Isis in Philae; Ptolemaic Period, second–first millennium BC.; sandstone

Architectural model
Small-scale models of architectural components were used in the Ptolemaic Period for training sculptors in traditional architectural forms. This lotus capital, rarely seen on buildings, has the pointed petals and round buds of a water lily.
Third–first millennium B.C.; limestone; Berlin, Ägyptisches Museum

Plant capital

The classical form of the papyrus capital bears a number of plant shapes. The papyrus and the lily embody the two halves of the country – Upper and Lower Egypt.

Columned Hall of the Temple of Isis on Philae; Ptolemaic-Roman Period; third century B.C.–third century A.D.; sandstone

Palm capital

Classical columnar forms maintained their place alongside the newly developed forms with floral composite capitals.
Columned Hall of the Temple of Isis on Philae; Ptolemaic-Roman Period; third century B.C.–third century A.D.; sandstone

Composite capital

The bundle of plants is interpreted here as a cylinder, but the capital is carved into many individual flower and leaf shapes.
Columned Hall of the Temple of Isis on Philae; Ptolemaic-Roman Period; third century B.C.–third century A.D.; sandstone

Houses for the Dead and Stairways to Heaven

Tomb Architecture of the Early Period

Page 23

Statue of King Djoser

King Djoser, for whom the Step Pyramid at Saqqara, the oldest monumental stone building in Egypt, was built, is here represented in a life-size statue of a seated figure. The statue was found in a statue chamber at the foot of the north face of the pyramid.
Old Kingdom, Dynasty III, c. 2500 B.C.; limestone, painted; Cairo, Egyptian Museum

The signature of Imhotep

On the base of a statue of King Djoser is the name of Imhotep, described as the "Chief Builder". In recognition of his achievements later generations raised him to the status of a god.
Old Kingdom, Dynasty III, c. 2650 B.C.; limestone; Cairo, Egyptian Museum

Abydos – Burial Place of the Founding Kings

The history of architecture in prehistoric Egypt has not yet been written, but if, one day, someone does venture such a work, then it will have to be based mainly on indirect sources, because hard archaeological evidence from this period is very rare. In scenes painted on vases in the fourth millennium B.C., we can see representations of shrines that give evidence of early tent-like or mud-brick constructions, and a few of the ornate relief palettes from the late prehistoric period depict architectural structures.

The type of tomb architecture so significant in all later epochs of Ancient Egypt is generally restricted up to the end of the fourth millennium B.C. to simple pits, probably lined with wood or matting, as can be deduced from archaeological evidence. Little is known about any superstructures that may also have been present. Thus we hesitate to speak of architecture in the commonly accepted sense.

It was not until around 3200 B.C. that richly equipped graves in several cemeteries began to incorporate underground chambers, lined with brick and fitted with a wooden beamed roof; these were probably the burial places of chiefs, the predecessors of the pharaohs. Apart from the main room in which the dead person lay in a wooden coffin, surrounded by rich gifts, there were also one or two side chambers with large numbers of containers for supplies, to provide for the deceased.

Around 3100 B.C. these underground brick tombs developed into the oldest type of royal tomb in Egypt. They are to be found in Abydos in Upper Egypt, which was the most important cult location for the worship of the god Osiris, and a religious centre throughout the history of Egypt. On the edge of the desert, far from the Nile valley, are the tombs of the pharaohs of Dynasty I (3000–2800 B.C.) and, as recent research in Abydos has shown, also those of the Dynasty immediately preceding this, Dynasty O (3100–3000 B.C.).

These tombs consist of broad pits dug into the ground, divided up into large rectangular chambers by means of solid brick walls. Most of the larger rooms have ancillary chambers leading off all four sides. Wooden beams were used for the ceilings and on the walls of the burial chambers, with stone slabs on some of the floors. A flight of steps leads from the outside of the tomb down into the underground complex, where the entrance is closed by large stone blocks. Superstructures would doubtless also have been built, but today we can only speculate as to their appearance. In Abydos they may have taken the form of a stylised burial mound, with slopes rising from a rectangular ground plan to a flat or slightly vaulted roof several metres above the ground. Close to the site funerary stelae of limestone or granite have been found with relief hieroglyphs bearing the names of the kings; these stelae probably stood inside the enclosing wall on the east side of the superstructures, facing the Nile valley and the rising sun.

Close to the cultivated land, about 1 km away to the north-east of these earliest royal tombs, and belonging to them, are giant brick complexes which are thought to be sites for the cult of the dead. Solid, niched brick walls encircle a wide, square court in which there were probably shrines and other cult structures made of material that easily degraded. The only break in this enclosing wall is a fortified gateway at the south-east corner. Wrongly called "forts", these complexes are clearly the precursors of the temple buildings in the pyramids of the Old Kingdom.

The niche element, a design feature also seen in prehistoric chamber tombs, is thought to have originally come from secular architecture, and used here it gives an insight into the function of the building, the architecture of the living was intended to provide the deceased with room for a continuation of life in the hereafter.

This basic Ancient Egyptian belief in the afterlife can also be clearly seen in the grave equipment placed in the tombs. Ivory and wooden models of houses show the wall arrangement and door construction of brick and wooden buildings, in anticipation of the typical decoration of coffins in the Old Kingdom and the Middle Kingdom.

The necropolis in the north of Saqqara provides rich archaeological material for the architecture of the Prehistoric Period. Its giant brick tombs are thought by the archaeologist W.B. Emery and many other scientists to be the actual royal tombs of the Early Dynastic Period, which means that the tombs in Abydos would take on the role of cenotaphs, of empty graves at the cult location for the worship of the god Osiris. However, the latest excavations in Abydos by the German Archaeological Institute have shown quite clearly that the Kings of Dynasties 0 and I were buried here. The graves in Saqqara are the resting-places of high dignitaries from the nearby town of Memphis, which is shown to have been in existence from the very early years of Egyptian history.

Not until about 2750 B.C. did Abydos lose its function as the traditional burial place of the pharaohs. From that point onwards the rulers of Egypt preferred a burial location near to their residence in Memphis. This move started a new tradition which led on to the Step Pyramid of Saqqara, the "Big 3" at Giza and through to the pyramids of the Kings in the Middle Kingdom in Dahshour, El-Lahun and Hawara.

The Djoser Complex in Saqqara

The funerary monument complex of King Djoser in Saqqara provides a most appropriate starting point for a survey of the architectural history of Ancient Egypt. It was built around 2650 B.C. and before this date the architecture of prehistoric and early dynastic Egypt can only be very sketchily reconstructed from secondary sources and scant archaeological evidence. Whereas here in Saqqara it now appears for the first time in stone and with precise detailing. Thanks to more than sixty years of research by Jean-Philippe Lauer, who to this day is tirelessly continuing his life's work of reconstructing the Djoser complex, the overall and detailed structure of this first monumental stone building in architectural history is wellknown. The line followed by Ancient Egyptian architecture in prehistoric and early dynastic Egypt finds full expression here in the Djoser complex.

The funerary complex of the king is surrounded by a niched wall (277 x 544 m), which seems to be an imitation of the mud-brick wall around the royal residence in Memphis, the aim being to provide the king with continued use of his palace in the hereafter. At the centre of the complex, high above the Nile on the rocky plateau of Saqqara, is the king's funerary monument, the Step Pyramid, which at about 70 m high far exceeded the scale of all previous Egyptian architecture. The partly destroyed south side of the seven-stepped pyramid allows us to see the inner structure of this first monumental stone building in Egypt. In the core of the Step Pyramid is a flat, rectangular structure corresponding to the mastaba tomb form, which, as an imitation in stone of a mud-brick house, formed the basic type of tomb in the Old Kingdom. The seven steps of the pyramid rising above this tomb exaggerate the form of the burial-mound of the graves of the kings of Abydos into a kind of "staircase to heavens" up which the king could rise into the heavenly hereafter. The house-type and the burial-mound type of tomb were typical of the settled and nomadic populations of Upper and Lower Egypt respectively, and by combining them in the architecture of the royal tomb they become a symbol of the two components

Oldest royal tombs in Abydos
The Kings of Dynasty I were buried in Abydos in Upper Egypt in enormous underground brick tombs. The above-ground structures, erected above the massive beamed ceiling of the chambers, have not survived.
C. 3000 B.C.

Step Pyramid of King Djoser
The technical and artistic evolution from the brick architecture of the early period to the monumental Step Pyramid of Djoser took place within just a few generations.
Old Kingdom, Dynasty III, c. 2650 B.C.

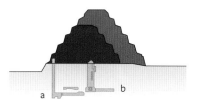

The Pyramid complex of Saqqara
The complex ensemble of buildings around the Step Pyramid is an imitation of the King's residence in Memphis, and as such was intended to surround him also in the next world. All the buildings are solid structures without internal rooms and therefore without any practical function.

  a. Tomb chamber
  b. Store rooms
  1. Niched wall
  2. Entrance hall
  3. South tomb
  4. Pyramid
  5. Ceremonial court
  6. South house
  7. North house
  8. Temple
  9. Altar
10. Court

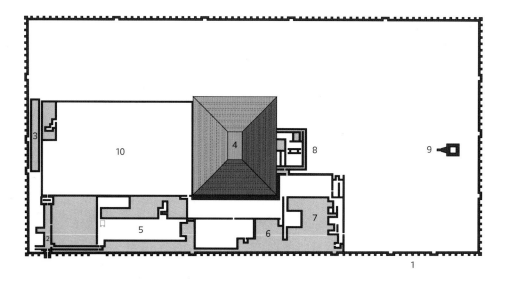

Enclosing wall around the Step Pyramid
Only a single gateway leads into the funerary complex of Djoser. The niched wall with bastion-like projections and recesses imitates the walls around the residence city of Memphis.
Old Kingdom, Dynasty III, c. 2650 B.C.; limestone

Page 33
Composite columns in the complex of Djoser
The composite columns in the entrance area are connected to each other or to the longitudinal walls via cross-walls. Expertise was not yet available in dealing with free-standing columns.
Old Kingdom, Dynasty III,
c. 2650 B.C.

Pyramid complex of King Djoser
All the buildings in the funerary complex of Djoser are representations in stone of real buildings of wood, mats and stone which stood in the residence city of Memphis.
Old Kingdom, Dynasty III,
c. 2650 B.C.

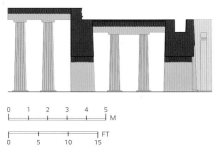

Cross-section of the entrance area
This cross-section of the entrance area clearly shows the roof construction. It consists of stone slabs placed on end, whereby the underside of each slab is half-rounded. This gives an impression of palm trunks spanning the space.

Plants as models for columns
The natural model of plant stems, grouped together to form a load-bearing column, can still be traced in the convex fluting of this stone pillar. The column is built up of small individual blocks and does not yet exploit the specific possibilities of stone architecture.
Entrance hall of the complex of Djoser; Old Kingdom, Dynasty III,
c. 2650 B.C.

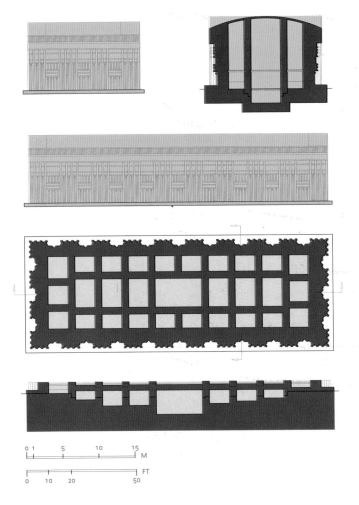

Southern enclosing wall of the Djoser complex
The niched wall around the funerary complex of King Djoser is 1.5 km long. Inside this wall is an extant representation in stone of what the royal residence of the Old Kingdom used to look like. Old Kingdom, Dynasty III, c. 2650 B.C.

Early Dynastic Period tomb in North Saqqara
Above: The tombs of high dignitaries in North Saqqara are hardly less impressive than the royal tombs in Abydos. Built in brick, they are a precursor of the stone architecture seen later in the Djoser complex.
Below: The many spatial divisions marked on the plan have no structural function, but instead they represent the many rooms for the use of the deceased.

Page 35 below
A wooden fence in stone
The areas in front of the shrines in the ceremonial court in the complex of Djoser were separated from each other by limestone walls which in relief depict a wooden fence.
Old Kingdom, Dynasty III, c. 2650 B.C.

Ceremonial court of the Djoser complex
The shrines in the ceremonial court are stone representations of lightweight, tent-like structures such as those erected for the gods of the individual districts at the King's jubilee celebrations. In the funerary complex they represent the eternal recurrence of this festival.
Old Kingdom, Dynasty III, c. 2650 B.C.

of the Egyptian state, under the King of Upper and Lower Egypt, as the pharaoh was known from early dynastic times.

Both grave types had already been combined in some brick graves in North Saqqara, where the outer form is that of a house-type tomb, but inside is an invisible core in the form of a burial mound. The niched enclosing wall of the Djoser group and the Step Pyramid itself are built of small limestone blocks, a design which is not ideal for the material, betraying its origins in brick architecture. This transfer of individual forms from secular architecture to royal tomb architecture can be seen throughout the Djoser complex. The entrance on the south-east corner of the enclosing wall (prefigured in the entrance to the brick complexes of the "forts" in Abydos) is covered with limestone slabs placed on end. The undersides of these slabs are rounded to look like palm-tree trunks lying next to one another, a roofing technique found in mud-brick architecture. The transition from the entrance gateway in the enclosing wall to the colonnade that leads to the court is formed by a high gateway with open doors. Made of limestone, the doors bear all the detailing found on real wooden door leaves – with door pins and swivel rings and beam reinforcement. The obtuse angle made between these immovable stone door leaves and the opening of the gateway gives the impression that the leaves can be swung, and as such is the expression in Ancient Egyptian architecture of a functioning door.

An unanswered question in archaeology is whether the niche structure of the 1.5 km long enclosing wall around the Djoser group was influenced by early brick architecture in Mesopotamia; what can be said, however, is that its material and labour-intensive type of construction is not a genuine form of stone architecture, but takes its cue purely from brick architecture. Both the complicated overall layout with its many individual buildings, and the detailing of these buildings, can be satisfactorily explained as the translation of secular buildings from the residence in Memphis into stone tomb architecture. The shrines either side of the ceremonial

The Upper Egyptian festival shrine
A lightweight construction of slim plant stems and a rushwork roof arching above is here translated into stone architecture, without losing any of its grace. This building is a solid "false" structure without any interior rooms. Djoser complex in Saqqara; Old Kingdom, Dynasty III, c. 2650 B.C.

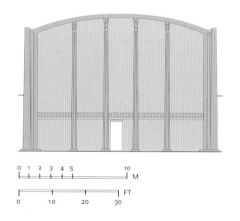

```
0 1 2 3 4 5          10
|-|-|-|-|-|----------|  M

|----------|----------|----------|  FT
0          10         20         30
```

Reconstruction of a tent shrine
The plant materials originally used for tent shrines can be traced in the form of the stone version constructed in the funerary complex.

court are copies of tent and brick structures that were built in the residence grounds as sacred sites for the various districts of Upper and Lower Egypt on the occasion of the king's jubilee of the renewal of kingship. Even the throne podium on which the king sat for the ceremonies is re-created here in stone.

The king himself, whose body is buried in a monolithic granite chamber deep below the Step Pyramid within a branching system of corridors, is represented in the form of statues near to the burial place. Standing figures, of which there were several incomplete examples around the temples, show him in a ceremonial cloak such as that worn for the jubilee celebrations, as a guarantee of never-ending rejuvenation; a seated figure was found in a statue-chamber on the north side of the pyramid, depicting the king looking out at the never-setting circumpolar stars. An inscription on one of the standing figures identifies the gifted creator of this earliest example of monumental stone architecture in Egypt as Imhotep, who in later centuries and millennia came to be worshipped as a cult hero, a saint and then finally as a god. This was indeed tremendous recognition for the emergence of Egypt into a new era of civilisation at the beginning of the third millennium B.C.

Statues of King Djoser in ceremonial dress
These unfinished statues of King Djoser show him a wearing knee-length cloak and holding a crosier and frond. As such these figures point to the function of the court in front of the shrines as the stage for an ever-recurring festival of kingship.
Old Kingdom, Dynasty III, ca. 2650 B.C.

Step Pyramid of Medum
This step pyramid was restyled by King Seneferu as a true pyramid.
Old Kingdom, Dynasties III/IV, c. 2600–2550 B.C.

"Red" (northern) pyramid of Dahshour
Built by King Seneferu as his second pyramid.
Old Kingdom, Dynasty IV, c. 2560 B.C.

The funerary complex of King Djoser in Saqqara marked the beginning of a period of almost explosive growth in architecture in Ancient Egypt. For the first time stone was the primary building material, and it heralded a technological revolution. That this new building material in religious architecture did not also bring with it a fundamental change in the language of architectural forms is one of the main characteristics of Egyptian art. The pictorial content of the building and its components and the primarily iconographic function of architecture remained largely untouched by technical advances.

However, the one significant exception to this was the pyramid. Its formal evolution from the Step Pyramid of Djoser to the classical form of the Pyramid of Cheops took place at a breathtakingly fast pace within the space of a single century, between 2650 to 2550 B.C.

The stages of this development can be seen very clearly in the example of the pyramid of Medum, erected in Dynasty III. Here, in the first and second phases of construction, the pyramid took the form of a step pyramid sloping upwards at an angle of 75°, but later the steps were filled in to give a smooth outline, but at a shallower angle of about 52°, in the classical pyramid shape. King Seneferu, in the latter years of whose reign this conversion took place, had already laid the groundwork for the discovery of the ideal pyramid form with his two pyramids in Dahshour, built in the decades before Medum. The Bent Pyramid at Dahshour, was intended as a real pyramid shape, but its angle of inclination was changed when it became clear that the 60° angle originally pursued would have led to a finished height of almost 140 m, an impossible feat. At about half-height the angle was therefore reduced to around 45°, bringing the final height down to 105 m. Seneferu's second pyramid, the "Red" pyramid in north Dahshour, was built from the start at the shallower angle. The angle of inclination of the third pyramid structure built by this king, the third phase of building in Medum, is also about 52° and as such is almost exactly the same as the Cheops pyramid. Almost all pyramids of the Old and Middle Kingdoms were then to model themselves, with little variation, on this classical forerunner in Medum.

The dimensions and proportions of the pyramids changed only when this purely royal tomb form was adapted for non-royal architecture. From the beginning of the New Kingdom in around 1550 B.C., steep-sided pyramids of only a few metres high began to be erected over private graves. In the necropolis in Thebes these miniature pyramids top the façades of rock-cut tombs and have east-facing niche openings containing a praying figure of the deceased, while in the necropolis in Memphis they are erected in the rear section of the temple-like tombs. In Saqqara in particular these private pyramids can be understood as a conscious reference to the towering royal pyramids of the Old and Middle Kingdoms which can be seen from Saqqara, as well as a reference to the building tradition manifest in them and to the historical and cultural heritage of their predecessors from ancient times.

The pyramid as a form of burial architecture for kings enjoyed an astounding renaissance in the Sudan for about a thousand years from 750 B.C. In the royal necropolises of El Kurru, Nuri, Gebel Barkal and Meroe there are well over 200 steep-sided pyramids, usually only 20 to 30 m high. They were probably modelled on the non-royal pyramid tombs of the New Kingdom, rather than on the royal graves in the far north in Giza and Saqqara.

Bent Pyramid of Dahshour
This pyramid was the first one built by King Seneferu. Technical and structural problems led to its angle of inclination being changed half-way through construction. Old Kingdom, Dynasty IV, c. 2570 B.C.

Bent Pyramid of Dahshour, plan and section
Not only was the angle of inclination changed during construction of the pyramid; the system of corridors and chambers also had to be modified due to structural damage.

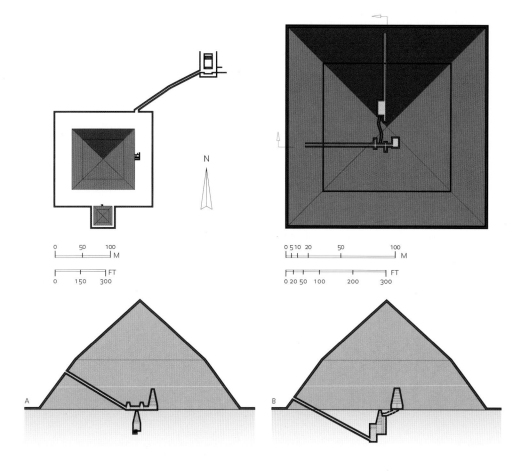

The Pyramid of Cheops
The largest Egyptian pyramid was almost 150 m high and as such is one of the largest structures ever built by man. Many questions concerning the technology and logistics of building this Wonder of the World are still unanswered.
Old Kingdom, Dynasty IV,
c. 2500 B.C.

Pyramids of Giza
In barely 100 years the step pyramid developed into the classical pyramid form, and to a size never achieved in later periods. The Pyramid of Chephren still has a portion of its original cladding. Next to the Pyramid of Mycerinus is one of the smaller ancillary pyramids.
Old Kingdom, Dynasty IV,
c. 2500–2465 B.C

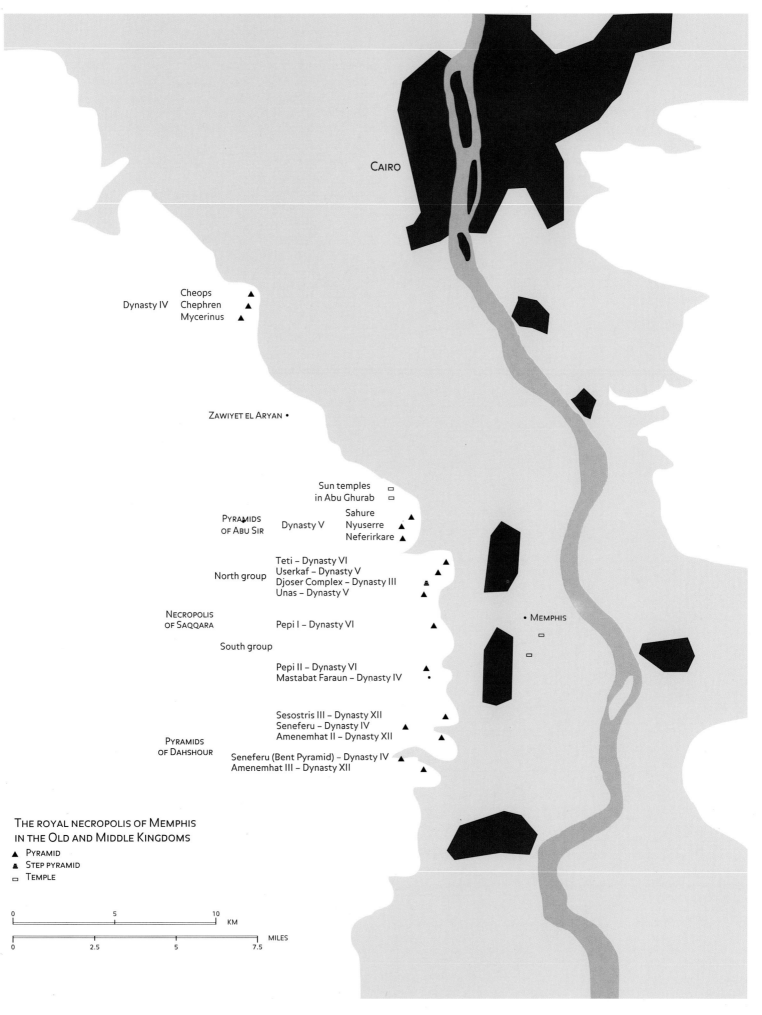

CAIRO

Dynasty IV — Cheops ▲
Chephren ▲
Mycerinus ▲

ZAWIYET EL ARYAN •

Sun temples ▢
in Abu Ghurab ▢

PYRAMIDS
OF ABU SIR — Dynasty V — Sahure ▲
Nyuserre ▲
Neferirkare ▲

Teti – Dynasty VI ▲
North group — Userkaf – Dynasty V ▲
Djoser Complex – Dynasty III ▲
Unas – Dynasty V ▲

NECROPOLIS
OF SAQQARA — Pepi I – Dynasty VI ▲

South group

Pepi II – Dynasty VI ▲
Mastabat Faraun – Dynasty IV •

• MEMPHIS
▢
▢

Sesostris III – Dynasty XII ▲
Seneferu – Dynasty IV ▲
Amenemhat II – Dynasty XII ▲

PYRAMIDS
OF DAHSHOUR — Seneferu (Bent Pyramid) – Dynasty IV ▲
Amenemhat III – Dynasty XII ▲

THE ROYAL NECROPOLIS OF MEMPHIS
IN THE OLD AND MIDDLE KINGDOMS
▲ PYRAMID
▲ STEP PYRAMID
▢ TEMPLE

0   5   10
               KM

0   2.5   5   7.5
               MILES

The Pyramid of Hawara
Originally clad in limestone, this brick structure is the second pyramid built by King Amenemhat III; the first, built in Dahshour, had structural faults which became evident even during the construction stage.
Middle Kingdom, Dynasty XII, c. 1800 B.C.

Burial pyramid in Deir el-Medinah
In the New Kingdom small, steep-sided pyramids were erected above the tombs of non-royal persons. Often a statue shrine was added on the eastern side.
New Kingdom, Dynasties XIX/XX, 1300–1100 B.C.

Pyramid in Meroe (Sudan)
In about 750 B.C. the Egyptian building style of the pyramid was adopted as a form for royal tombs in the Sudan. This style continued here for a further thousand years. On the eastern side of the pyramid is a sacrificial shrine with pylon.
Meroitic Period, c. A.D. 155–170

Page 43
The royal cemetery of Meroe
From about 270 B.C.–A.D. 320 the kings and queens of the Meroitic kingdom had their pyramid tombs built in the desert, on the mountains to the east of the town, where hundreds of years before members of the royal family had been buried in small pyramids.

BUILDING FOR THE LIFE TO COME

Old Kingdom Pyramids

Giza

In around 2500 B.C., only 100 years after the construction of the Step Pyramid group of King Djoser in Saqqara, pyramid architecture reached its quantitative and qualitative peak in the Great Pyramid of King Cheops in Giza. Its original height of 146.5 m and the 230 m sides make it the largest of the Egyptian pyramids. Regarded in ancient times as one of the Seven Wonders of the World, it has lost none of its fascination to this day. Many investigations of its archaeology, construction and metrology have been conducted, and countless pseudo-scientific attempts made to explain its significance, but nevertheless the architectural achievement represented by the Pyramid of Cheops still escapes our intellectual grasp. The system of corridors and chambers in the pyramid's interior has been examined in great detail, and their function explained partly in terms of technical requirements (the Great Gallery as a storeroom for the plug-blocks used to close the entrance to the tomb chamber), and partly in terms of religious motives (the "ventilation shafts" as paths for the soul of the king in his eternal afterlife), yet fundamental questions still remain unanswered, in particular concerning construction technology and the transport of building materials.

Ramps and sleds with wide runners were almost certainly used in positioning the limestone blocks brought from the quarries and the granite ashlars for the sarcophagus chambers. Some of these blocks weighed up to 40 tons and were transported for 800 km on the Nile from Aswan. Depending on the size of the pyramid and the height to be reached at the various stages of construction, it was probable that a range of different types of ramps were used. Smooth, wide ramps with a low angle of slope enabled a large number of workers to be used on the lower levels, whereas for work on the upper layers, ramps with steps and lifting gear were probably used. The spiral ramp winding round the centre of the pyramid would have been unsuitable for moving heavy loads. There is archaeological evidence of an internal ramp which projected deep into the structure of the building, and which at its lower levels was used for shifting material. It is, however, pointless to speculate about which types of ramps were used for the various pyramids; this can only be established through careful investigation on site. Any theory claiming to have found the answer as to how the Ancient Egyptians solved the transport problems in building all pyramids is to be treated with suspicion in the present state of our archaeological knowledge.

It is almost impossible to reach an understanding of the overall Cheops complex, as only very little remains of the temple structures to the east of the pyramid; even the name of its royal patron is not in evidence. A single, tiny ivory figure from Abydos bears his name, and historical inscriptions from the period of his reign are almost totally absent.

Close to the Pyramid of Cheops, on slightly higher ground, is the Pyramid of Chephren, built a few decades later and, at 143.5 m high, the second largest pyramid in Egypt. Much of this pyramid, together with its temple structures, is consid-

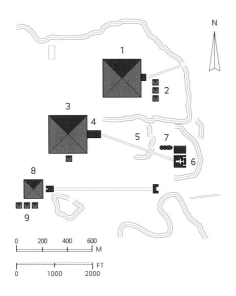

The pyramid site at Giza
Within the space of a few decades between 2500 and 2465 B.C. the "Big Three" were created – the Pyramids of Cheops, Chephren and Mycerinus (from north to south) along with temple buildings and ancillary pyramids.
1. Pyramid of Cheops
2. Pyramids nearby
3. Pyramid of Chephren
4. Temple of the Dead
5. Causeway corridor
6. Valley Temple
7. Sphinx
8. Pyramid of Mycerinus
9. Pyramids nearby

The Pyramids of Chephren and Cheops
Because it stands on slightly higher ground the Pyramid of Chephren seems larger than the Pyramid of Cheops (in the background), which has lost its cap. Arrayed around the pyramids are the mastaba tombs of the members of the royal household.
Old Kingdom, Dynasty IV, c. 2500–2465 B.C.

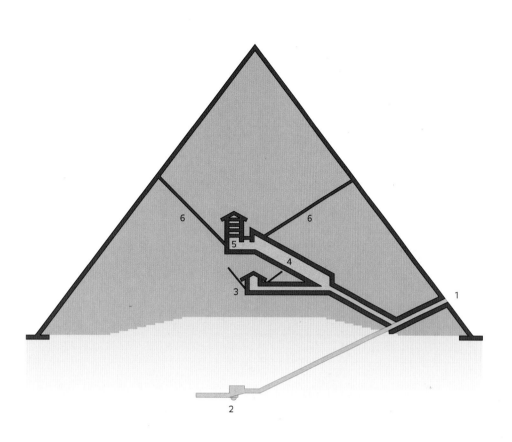

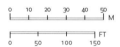

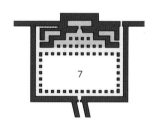

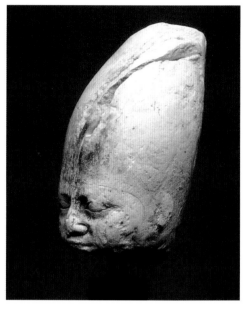

Head of a statue of a king
The small head wearing the crown
of Upper Egypt can be dated on
stylistic evidence to the beginning
of Dynasty IV. It is not certain
whether the king is Seneferu or
Cheops.
Old Kingdom, Dynasty IV,
c. 2500 B.C.; limestone; Munich,
Staatliche Sammlung Ägyptischer
Kunst

**Section through the Pyramid of
Cheops and plan of the pyramid
temple of Cheops**
Above: It has not yet been fully explained why this pyramid has three
chambers. The construction plans
may have been altered during
building, or they may have been
planned from the outset as three
separate functional elements.

Below: The ground plan of this
completely destroyed temple can
only be reconstructed from evidence of construction in the basalt
paving. 1. Entrance, 2. Uncom-
pleted room, 3. Central room,
4. Great Gallery, 5. Sarcophagus
room, 6. Air channels, 7. Mortuary
temple

Pyramid-building techniques

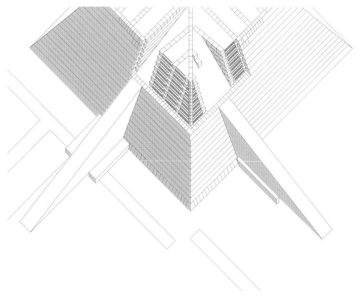

Techniques of transport

Another unsolved question is how hundreds of thousands of blocks, some weighing several tons, were transported. Ramps were used for the lower part of the structure and various theories have been put forward to explain this technique. It is not known how the transport problem was solved for the upper part of the pyramids.

Building ramps on the First Pylon of the Temple of Amun in Karnak

The last extension project in the 2000 year history of building at the Temple of Amun remained unfinished. During a period of political change the First Pylon was left as a building site. Remains of building ramps can still be seen on the back of the pylon. Such ramps were used to transport building material.
Ptolemaic Period

The procedure of pyramid-building

The inner structure of the pyramids of the Old Kingdom is still largely unknown. It is probable that from the start of Dynasty IV, the porous limestone core blocks were built up in horizontal layers, with the cladding of thick limestone blocks being positioned as building progressed.

Page 53

Levelled site for the Pyramid of Chephren
Large areas of the slightly inclined rocky plateau around the Pyramid of Chephren were levelled to create a flat site for building. Large square stone blocks were hewn out of the limestone face. Old Kingdom, Dynasty IV, c. 2500 B.C.

The Great Gallery in the Pyramid of Cheops
A huge hall with corbel vault was created inside of the pyramid to hold the plug-blocks which were dropped into position from the inside to block off the corridors leading up to the chamber with the King's body.
From: Luigi Mayer, *Views in Egypt,* 1804

erably better preserved than the Cheops burial complex. Around the top of the pyramid its original, smooth-polished limestone cladding can still be seen, and at the base some of the granite cladding has also been preserved. On the north and west sides of the pyramid the solid rocky ground on which it stands bears many traces of measurements and building preparations, enabling conclusions to be drawn about construction planning and procedures. All the key components of the temple complex on the east side of the pyramid are recognisable: the mortuary temple itself with open court and five sanctuaries is built very close to the pyramid and reached by a 500 m long causeway corridor hewn from solid rock. The causeway, with its high rock walls, begins on the edge of the cultivated land at the Chephren Valley Temple, a unique structure in Ancient Egyptian architecture. Here, behind temple walls made of limestone and several metres thick, is a T-shaped hall with walls clad with giant granite blocks; the ceiling, of granite beams, rests on mono-

Tip of the Pyramid of Chephren in Giza
Originally this pyramid was clad with fine, polished limestone from Tura which emphasised the crystalline precision of the architecture. On the Pyramid of Chephren the uppermost part of the cladding has survived.
Old Kingdom, Dynasty IV, c. 2500 B.C.

Pyramid of Chephren in Giza
The angle of inclination of the Giza pyramids perfectly combines the earthliness of the construction with a dynamic striving upwards towards the heavens, to which the dead king was to rise via the "stairway to heaven" formed by the pyramid.
Old Kingdom, Dynasty IV, c. 2500 B.C.

lithic granite pillars. The total lack of wall decoration and the stereometric basic forms of this room speak of an abstract rigour which is completely at odds with the fundamental naturalistic tendencies of Egyptian architecture. Placed in front of the red granite walls on bright white calcite and alabaster flooring were twenty-three statues of the king in grey-green gneiss, dimly lit through narrow openings at the top of the walls.

Next to the valley temple is another temple complex which was probably built at the same time and may have a connection with the monumental Sphinx. This figure, depicting the god-like characteristics of the king, is 70 m long and 20 m high, and is the largest sculpture in Ancient Egypt.

The temple complex next to the third and smallest of the Giza pyramids, built by Mycerinus, was unfinished and in part constructed only of mud bricks. The pyramid cladding of granite blocks was also unfinished.

Valley Temple of the Pyramid of Chephren
The core masonry of the valley temple consists of huge blocks of local limestone. They are clad with granite which was transported to the site from Aswan, about 800 km away. No two blocks, and therefore no two joints, are the same shape, as each quarried block was hewn to the shape best suited to its individual volume.
Old Kingdom, Dynasty IV, c. 2500 B.C.

Statue group with King Mycerinus
In the unfinished Valley Temple of the Pyramid of Mycerinus there were several statue groups showing the king in close connection with Hathor, the goddess of the heavens, and with a local divinity who embodied the forces of the earth.
Old Kingdom, Dynasty IV,
c. 2500 B.C.; greywacke;
Cairo, Egyptian Museum

Pyramid of Mycerinus in Giza
The smallest of the three pyramids in Giza, the Pyramid of King Mycerinus, was originally clad entirely in red granite. The pyramid was never completed; the only granite surfaces to be polished were those around the entrance to the inner pyramid.
Old Kingdom, Dynasty IV,
c. 2500 B.C.

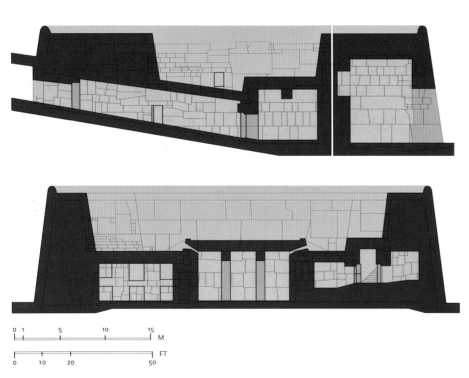

0 1   5   10   15
|—|—|——|——|——| M

|—|——|——|————————| FT
0   10   20   50

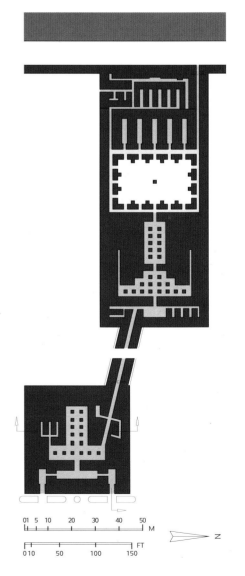

01 5 10   20   30   40   50
|—|—|—|——|——|——|——| M

|—|————|————|————| FT
010   50   100   150

⊳—— z

Longitudinal and cross-section through the Valley Temple of Chephren
Behind the granite cladding are massive limestone blocks, in the middle of which is the pillared hall. Light enters this space through angled window slits. The slope of the causeway corridor begins in this inner temple area.

Plan of the Valley Temple of Chephren
Twenty-three seated figures of the king were found in the temple's pillared hall. A causeway corridor, almost 500 m long, leads to the mortuary temple with pillared hall, long hall, statue courtyard and five statue shrines. Beyond these are the store-rooms.

Page 57
Valley Temple of the Pyramid of Chephren
The clarity of form of the pillars in the Valley Temple of the Pyramid of Chephren is often regarded as typically Egyptian. However, this is in fact very much an exception, as the basic principle of Egyptian architecture is that buildings in stone imitated the forms seen in structures made of wood, mats and bricks.
Old Kingdom, Dynasty IV, c. 2500 B.C.

The Sphinx of Giza
The Sphinx of Giza is 73.5 m long and the largest monumental statue of Ancient Egypt. Framed by a headdress the head of the king looks east to the rising sun. The facial characteristics of this statue are in the same style as that of the statues of the successors of Cheops, the Kings Radedef and Chephren.
Old Kingdom, Dynasty IV, c. 2550–2500 B.C.; limestone

Page 59
The Sphinx of Giza
A lion's body and a human head combine in the figure of the sphinx to show the king in divine form, as the "son of Re", the direct offspring of the sun-god. This colossal figure is hewn from a rocky outcrop. All around the sphinx this area has been quarried to provide stone for building the pyramids.
Old Kingdom, Dynasty IV, c. 2550–2500 B.C.; limestone

Abu Sir

The mysterious silence surrounding the "Big 3" at Giza in Dynasty IV (2575–2465 B.C.), arising from the lack of any substantial pictorial or textual evidence, was followed in Dynasty V (2465–2325 B.C.) by the royal pyramid complexes in Abu Sir, which answered many of the questions left open by Giza. In Abu Sir, lying between Giza and Saqqara and within sight of both, are the funerary complexes of the four Kings Sahure, Neferirkare, Neferefre and Nyuserre.

The Sahure pyramid complex, excavated at the beginning of the twentieth century by Ludwig Borchardt, is well preserved and gives a representative picture of a royal burial site in the Old Kingdom.

The valley temple is located on the edge of the cultivated land and was connected to the Nile by a causeway, probably dug to transport building materials. The causeway, part of which had an artificial embankment, was bordered by high walls, on top of which lay a roof of giant slabs of limestone. A narrow slit between the slabs allowed faint light to filter through into the causeway and onto the relief friezes placed one above the other along both walls. The total length of the friezes reaches several kilometres. A dominant theme in them is the political and dogmatic position of the Egyptian king in the world. Egypt's enemies, the Nubians in the south, Libyans in the west, Asians in the east, are seen as bound prisoners being brought before the king. This picture of the world as it was perceived by the pharaohs was supplemented by a representation of the order of the cosmos in nature. Plump, hermaphroditic beings, the Nile gods, join female gods in carrying offering plates from which are suspended symbols of life; in the accompanying inscriptions these gods are called "food", "water" and "corn", and thus represent the fertility of the Nile valley. Other relief pictures seem to depict historical events, such as the one show-

Pyramid temple of King Sahure in Abu Sir
The causeway corridor leads from the valley temple to the mortuary temple. Palmiform columns once stood in the court. The inner temple rooms lead to the statue hall and to a false door at the foot of the pyramid.
Old Kingdom, Dynasty V, c. 2450 B.C.

Page 61 above
Pyramid complex at Abu Sir
Half-way between Saqqara in the south and Giza in the north is the pyramid complex of the kings of Dynasty V at Abu Sir. From the top of the Pyramid of Sahure we can see the Pyramids of Neferirkare (right) and Nyuserre (left). The pyramids in Abu Sir were built only a few generations after the ones in Giza, but they lack the technical perfection of the latter.
Old Kingdom, Dynasty V, c. 2450 B.C.

Plan of the pyramid site at Abu Sir
Close to the royal burial complexes of the Pyramids of Sahure, Nyuserre and Neferirkare (from north to south) are several other pyramids, some of which have not yet been fully excavated. The architectural complex at Abu Sir arose over a particular period of time and is one of exceptional density.

A Pyramid complex of King Sahure
   1. Valley Temple, 2. Causeway corridor, 3. Mortuary temple, 4. Pyramid

B Pyramid complex of King Nyuserre
   1. Valley Temple, 2. Causeway corridor, 3. Mortuary temple, 4. Pyramid

C Pyramid complex of King Neferirkare
   1. Mortuary temple, 2. Pyramid

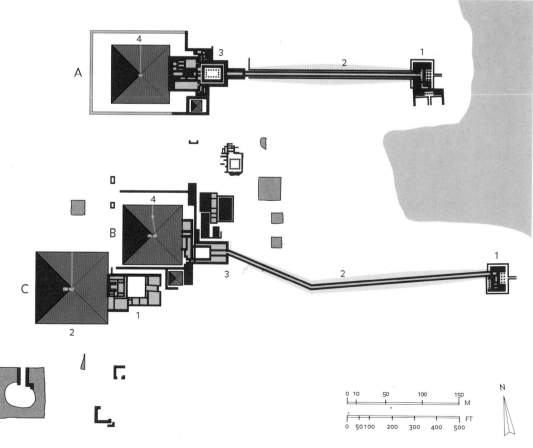

The god Sopdu

The walls of the causeway corridor from the valley temple to the mortuary temple of the Pyramid of Sahure were decorated with several hundred metres of reliefs, some of which depicted Egyptian gods delivering captured enemies to the king. The beard and distinctive cheekbones of the god Sopdu, the "Lord of Foreign Lands", are characteristic of people from the Near East. Old Kingdom, Dynasty V, c. 2450 B.C.; limestone; Berlin, Ägyptisches Museum

The god Seth

While Sopdu protects the eastern border of Egypt, the aardvaark-headed Seth is the protective deity for Upper Egypt. In his hands he holds a battleaxe and a rope for tying up enemies. Above him is the starry sky, linking political events with the divine realm.
Relief in the Sahure complex causeway corridor; Old Kingdom, Dynasty V, c. 2450 B.C.; limestone; Berlin, Ägyptisches Museum

Gods of fertility
Female and hermaphroditic figures carry before them sacrificial plates from which hang symbols of life. The inscriptions for water, corn and food identify the figures as divine personifications of the fertility of the Nile valley. These reliefs were part of a picture frieze mounted around the base of the walls in the temple court of the Pyramid of Sahure.
Old Kingdom, Dynasty V, c. 2450 B.C.; limestone; Cairo, Egyptian Museum

ing large trading ships returning from the Near East, or the stone blocks (only discovered in 1994) with relief figures of emaciated Bedouins or Libyan chiefs and their families bringing tributes. Similar, sometimes almost identical, relief scenes can, however, also be found in other royal temple complexes from the Old Kingdom. These scenes can thus be regarded as standard items which do not tell of single incidents, but are more generalised in content. The focus was not the specific ruler at a particular time, but pharaohs in general.

The causeway ends in an open court which is surrounded by monolithic palmiform columns of red granite. The roof of this portico has a star pattern, mimicking the vault of the heavens above the open court space. The black basalt paving on the courtyard is the same colour as the fertile agricultural land in the Nile valley. Thus the paving, the pillars and the roof together form an architectural cosmos, a world picture in stone. At the junction of earth and heaven, on the architraves above the palmiform capitals, are the names of the king. He is the link between man and god; he creates divine order on earth, an order which finds its visible and lasting expression in the architecture of the temple.

In Abu Ghurab, not far from Abu Sir the Kings of Dynasty V erected sun temples which exclusively serve this representation of the man-god relationship in the person and function of the king. Their composition is similar to that of the pyramid temples in that they have a valley structure, a causeway corridor and a temple, but they have no pyramid. Instead, a compact obelisk made of stone blocks stands on a pyramid stump in the wide temple courtyard. In this monument to the cult of the sun-god Re the incarnation of god in the figure of the king is manifested.

In King Nyuserre's temple to the sun-god in Abu Ghurab, the walls of the causeway corridor leading from the valley structure to the obelisk are decorated with relief cycles showing the jubilee of the renewal of kingship, in which he experiences cyclically recurring rejuvenation. The most interesting relief pictures, however, are the representations of life in nature. Organised into seasons, they depict animals procreating and being born, migrating birds and fish swimming up the Nile to spawn. These famous "Season Reliefs" are a picture hymn to the sun-god, a precursor to the sun song of Akhenaten or that of Francis of Assisi.

Inscriptions state that sun temples were built for six kings of Dynasty V, but only those of Sahure and Nyuserre have been identified and excavated. The divine nature of the Egyptian king, as represented by the architecture of these temples, is not bound to the individual person of the respective ruler, but to the institution of kingship. The king as a person is mortal, and therefore special mechanisms for transfiguration are required for his continued existence in the hereafter. The pyramid is a staircase to the heavens, enabling the king to rise up to the gods, an idea which is easily recognised in the early form of the step pyramid.

In the texts which have been chiselled into the walls of the underground chambers in the pyramids since Dynasty V, the king describes his journey to the heavens: "You have your heart, Osiris; you have your legs, Osiris; you have your arms, Osiris. Thus so, too, do I have my heart, my legs, my arms. A staircase to the heavens has been built for me, so that I can rise up into heaven, and I rise up on great clouds of smoke. I fly up as a bird, I alight as a beetle on the empty throne that is in your barque, Re!" As for the purpose of this journey to heaven, we learn, "The doors of heaven will be opened to you, you will emerge from them as Horus." The king, who like Osiris is eternal, reaches heaven via a staircase, and this journey is accompanied by the sacrificial smoke of the funerary rituals.

The temple complex is the stage for the funerary cult, serving both the physical requirements of the dead king and his ritual transfiguration. The architectural form and wall decoration of the burial chambers in these pyramids are a reflection of such

Relief from the Sun Temple of Nyuserre
Several kings of Dynasty V built sun temples close to their pyramids. In these temples they entered into close union with the sungod, Re. A relief cycle in the Sun Temple of Nyuserre shows the influence of Re on nature – a picture hymn to the sun.
Old Kingdom, Dynasty V, c. 2400 B.C.; limestone; Berlin, Ägyptisches Museum

Burial chamber in the Pyramid of Unas

The gabled roof is decorated with stars, and the walls around the coffin have relief decoration in imitation of mat hangings. The burial chamber is both a representation of the home of the deceased and of his surroundings in the next world. The king rests in the centre of a world consisting of earthly reminiscences and divine hopes. Old Kingdom, Dynasty V, c. 2350 B.C.

King Sahure

This statue depicts Sahure in royal headdress and with a king's beard. Sahure was the king for whom the first pyramid in Abu Sir was built. The type of stone from which this statue is made was also used by King Chephren for his statues. Old Kingdom, Dynasty IV., c. 2450 B.C.; anorthosite gneiss; New York, The Metropolitan Museum of Art

ideas: under a starry gabled roof, representing the heavenly afterworld of the king, stands the monolithic stone sarcophagus of the ruler in the middle of a room with walls decorated with carpet patterns; they turn the burial chamber into a richly appointed hall in the palace, thus turning the secular into the sacred, the transitory into the eternal.

Relief of Mereruka in Saqqara
The practice of combining front
and side views in Ancient Egyptian
relief pictures lends the human
figure a depth of space which is
enhanced into three dimensions
by the expanse of the wall.
Old Kingdom, Dynasty VI,
c. 2300 B.C.

**Sacrificial hall in the tomb of
Mereruka**
A vividly carved statue of the
deceased steps out of the mock
door at the top of the burial shaft,
marking the threshold between
this world and the next. At the
feet of the statue, on top of a
flight of steps, is the stone table
on which sacrifices were made.
The wall reliefs depict an idealised
view of life on earth.
Old Kingdom, Dynasty VI,
c. 2300 B.C.

Tomb relief of Huti
The central motif of the tomb reliefs in the Old Kingdom is a representation of the deceased at the table of offerings, or sacrificial table. Shown on it are rounds of bread and around it are hieroglyphs of other offerings. The tomb is the deceased's house and as such the place where he meets his family and descendants.
From Tomb B 9 in Saqqara; Old Kingdom, Dynasty IV/V, 2500–2400 B.C.; limestone; Cairo, Egyptian Museum

Old Kingdom Tombs

Two sets of ideas come together in the king's tomb, the pyramid and its temple complexes. The afterlife of the king is in part a continuation of his life on earth, but primarily an ascent from the earthly to the heavenly. Ordinary people are denied this ascent. For them hopes of life in the hereafter were limited to an idealised continuation of earthly conditions. Accordingly tomb architecture reflected this belief, the tombs being the eternal houses of the deceased. The elaborate wall decoration of private tombs in Dynasty III contains relief and painted pictures of sumptuously appointed living rooms with woven mats and colourful carpets. The outer form of the tomb and the rectangular ground plan with sloping walls takes up the forms of traditional mud-brick architecture. This typical form gave rise to the name "mastaba", an Arabic word for the stockpile of mud bricks up against the houses.

On the east side of these mastabas there are usually two doors; however, as the burial mound itself is immediately behind them, they cannot really be opened and are called false doors. The false doors are functionally the most important part of the tomb, because the communication between this world and the next takes place through them. In front of the doors was placed a sacrificial slab, on which the descendants of the deceased were to place offerings of food. The deceased could climb up from the burial chamber deep down inside the mound where his body lay in a wooden or stone coffin, and enter the cult chamber through the door. In some tombs this to-ing and fro-ing between the two worlds through the false door is very specifically depicted; a high-relief, sculpted figure of the deceased is shown on the door itself, very impressively in the case of Mereruka's tomb in Saqqara. In the tomb of Idu in Giza shown on the lower part of the false door is the upper body of the deceased, creating the impression that he is just emerging from the tomb shaft leading from the burial chamber upwards to the cult chamber.

The two parts of the tomb are functionally and spatially strictly separate, but meet at the false door – on the one side the inaccessible underground burial area, consisting of the burial chamber and a shaft that was filled after the burial, and on the other a ground-level cult area accessible to the descendants for pursuance of the funerary cult. The false door itself also displays elements of typical mud-brick forms in its posts and half-round cross-member in the shape of a palm-tree trunk or a bundle of rushes, such as is used for lintels in mud-brick structures. Often the door is framed with roll moulding and a cavetto, the basic elements of mud-brick houses.

Statue of Seneb and his family
In the above-ground part of the tomb were statues of those buried deep below in the underground part of the tomb. The statue is placed in the *serdab,* a totally enclosed chamber out of sight of the visitor to the tomb. In some tombs this chamber is linked to the sacrificial chamber by means of narrow peepholes in the wall. The statue of the dwarf Seneb, his wife and two children was found in a stone box with a closed lid.
Old Kingdom. Dynasty IV, c. 2450 B.C.; limestone; Cairo, Egyptian Museum

During the period of the Old Kingdom the original compact mass of the mastaba developed into a range of interior rooms, becoming in its spatial arrangement more like a real house for the dead, sometimes even taking the form of a whole complex of buildings containing the tombs of several family members. The position of the mastaba tombs in the residence cemeteries of Giza, Abu Sir and Saqqara reflects the social status of the occupant. Members of the royal family and the highest-ranking state officials had their tombs erected closest to the royal pyramid complex, the lower ranks being buried progressively further away. In spatial organisation, too, these cemeteries are mirror-images of earthly reality. The mastabas lie in regularly laid out streets, encroaching only at their extremities into the proliferating suburbs. It is not so much the architecture of the mastabas of the Old Kingdom that makes them an invaluable component in the archaeology of Ancient Egypt, but above all the relief and painted wall decoration. From the outside these tombs are generally quite without ornament, but after passing through the tomb entrance, with carvings of the deceased in hollow relief on the doorposts, a very vivid world of pictures

Old Kingdom burial complex
The actual burial chamber lies below ground at the bottom of a vertical shaft cut into the rock. The shaft was filled in after interment. Originally there may have been a portrait head of the deceased (see arrow) in a recess in the corridor. The above-ground structures were called "mastabas" because of their banked sides (*mastaba* means "bank" in Arabic). At the beginning of the Old Kingdom, these mastabas were in the form of solid stone hills, but later they developed into houses for the dead, with as many as sixty rooms.

is revealed on the walls of the rooms inside. Apart from the lower part of the walls, hardly any space is left undecorated.

These wall pictures, mostly in painted low-relief carvings, but seldom purely painting alone, seem at first to make no reference to religious themes. They depict in inexhaustible detail the many aspects of daily life, with scenes from agriculture, the workshops of the artisans, as well as sporting, hunting and boating scenes. These images are a rich source of iconographic information, almost like a kind of handbook of Ancient Egyptian cultural history. Representations of gods are totally lacking here, and yet these everyday scenes are part of a primarily religiously motivated pictorial programme. The focus of the scenes is the deceased, before whom an ideal reality unfolds in the pictures, a vision of eternity that is an exaggeration of normal life. As a seated figure, enthroned, he is present in the inaccessible part of the tomb, taking his part in the picture. The central image in the tomb reliefs is found on top of or near the false door: the deceased, now transfigured, as evidenced by his enthronement, is seated at the sacrificial table, reaching for the offerings piled up in front of him, a list of which is recorded in the accompanying hieroglyphic inscription. As a complement to the relief pictures of the deceased on the doorposts, in which he is depicted walking, are statues of a standing, walking figure, which guarantee him his physical capabilities in the afterlife. Both aspects, transfiguration and continuation of his physical existence are essential prerequisites for eternal life.

A special form of tombs in the Old Kingdom are the rock-cut tombs. Depending on their particular location, they are either partly or wholly hewn out of a rocky outcrop and in many cases seem to make use of available cave-like spaces left by underground quarrying. In the quarry areas of Central Egypt this tomb form became very popular for the provincial necropolises during the Middle Kingdom. In the New Kingdom it finally became the only tomb type.

Apart from reasons of pragmatism, the rock-cut tombs of the Old Kingdom may also have reflected an idea which was to become evident in the New Kingdom, namely that tomb spaces under the ground reach out from the known world into unknown regions, they are the architecturally designed path into the beyond, and therefore already have religious content in their architectural form.

Tomb relief of Metjetji

In the technique of hollow relief, the background around the figures is not carved out, but stands proud. The figures are cut into the wall. The deeply-cut contours cast a strong shadow which made this relief technique particularly popular for the outer walls of tombs and temples.

From Saqqara; Old Kingdom, Dynasty V, c. 2400 B.C.; limestone; Berlin, Ägyptisches Museum

THE LOST CLASSICAL PERIOD

Architecture of the Middle Kingdom

Page 73

Mirror handle

The architectural element of the plant column with papyrus capital has been adopted here for a mirror-handle. The face of the goddess Hathor is integrated in the papyrus umbel. Her animal form can be seen in the cow's ears.
From El-Lahun; Middle Kingdom, Dynasty XII, c. 1800 B.C.; gold, obsidian, semi-precious stones; Cairo, Egyptian Museum

Head of a statue of King Sesostris III

Statues in the Middle Kingdom expressed the individuality of the ruler, which makes it possible to identify even those statues which bear no inscription.
From Karnak; Middle Kingdom, Dynasty XII, c. 1830–1820 B.C.; granite; Luxor, Luxor Museum

Temples of the Gods and Rock Tombs

The architectural tradition of the royal pyramid tombs of the Old Kingdom ended with the decline of Memphis as the country's capital. The Old Kingdom collapsed and during reunification in the First Intermediate Period around 2050 B.C. the Upper Egyptian town of Thebes rose in significance, also marking the rise of a region of the Nile valley that had previously had very little influence. Now it became the motor behind new impulses in art and architecture.

Although mastaba tombs from the Early Dynastic Period have been found in the northern part of Thebes, in El Tarif, tomb architecture in the early Middle Kingdom pursued new directions. The political and military elite at the court of the king who united the nation, Mentuhotep II (2040–2010 B.C.) had their tombs built on the western bank at Thebes as rock-cut tombs in the valley basin of Deir el-Bahari, either high up on the outcrop, or in the Assasif valley. The king also chose the same burial location, perhaps influenced by the ancient cave shrine of the goddess Hathor.

Mentuhotep's tomb is quite different to the pyramid complexes of the Old Kingdom. The king is no longer entombed in the middle of a monumental stairway to the heavens, up which he can climb to the gods, but lies buried 150 m deep in the mountainside. In front of this underworld part of the tomb is built a terrace on which a stylised hill rises on a square ground plan – it is a picture of the creation of the world, in which the holy grove just below the terrace probably also plays its part. Only the valley temple and the causeway corridor are a reminder of the traditional tomb structure of the pyramid complexes of the Old Kingdom. The front part of the terrace temple is dedicated to the cult of the gods Montu and Amun, with whom the king identified himself, a concept not dissimilar to the sun temples of Dynasty V.

At the same time, on the east bank of the Nile, there were the beginnings of a temple complex which within the space of a few decades would become the most important shrine in Egypt, a position it was to maintain until the end of the pharaonic period. The shrine was Karnak, dedicated to Amun-Re, soon to become known as the "King of the gods". In the course of two millennia Karnak continued to grow until it became a temple city, but the site of the oldest, most venerable shrine in the complex was always kept free from new building. Of this temple only the granite thresholds slab of a sequence of several gates have survived; the temple itself was probably initially constructed of mud bricks and faced the Nile. Of the Middle Kingdom buildings around this "court of the Middle Kingdom", which is not in fact a courtyard, but the site of the original temple of Karnak, little has been preserved, but enough to be able to document the very quick growth of this new temple to the gods.

The most significant Middle Kingdom building in Karnak is the "White Chapel" of King Sesostris I (1971–1926 B.C.). Just 6.5 x 6.5 m in size, this structure was originally built for the king's jubilee and located close to the Temple of Amun-Re in Karnak, but had to be dismantled to make way for extensions to nearby buildings,

Mortuary temple of King Mentuhotep II in Deir el-Bahari
As in the pyramid complexes of the Old Kingdom, a long causeway corridor led from a valley temple directly to the mortuary temple of Mentuhotep at the foot of the vertical rock-face of Deir el-Bahari. Standing and seated statues of the king were placed between trees along an avenue in the wide court in front of the tomb. We can see the beds in which the trees were planted to this day.
Middle Kingdom, Dynasty XI, c. 2400 B.C.

The temples of Deir el-Bahari
The terrace temple (foreground) of Queen Hatshepsut was built in 1470 B.C. Its style, with two terrace levels, mimics that of the Temple of Mentuhotep II (background), built more than 500 years earlier. From the innermost part of the Temple of Mentuhotep a long passageway leads westward down into the king's tomb deep inside the mountain.

Mortuary temple of King Mentuhotep II in Deir el-Bahari
The royal mortuary temple is surrounded by the rock-cut tombs of high dignatories. These tombs, with their steep outer courts are situated on the slopes to the north and south of the temple and also in front of it, cut into the rocky valley bottom.
Middle Kingdom, Dynasty XI, c. 2040 B.C.

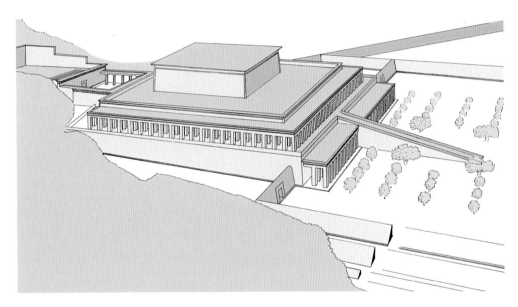

Reconstruction of the mortuary temple of King Mentuhotep
Surrounded by several rows of four-cornered and eight-cornered pillars, a kind of stylised primeval hill emerged as the image of the creation of the world and the daily rebirth of the sun. The temple is oriented to the point on the horizon from which the sun rises.

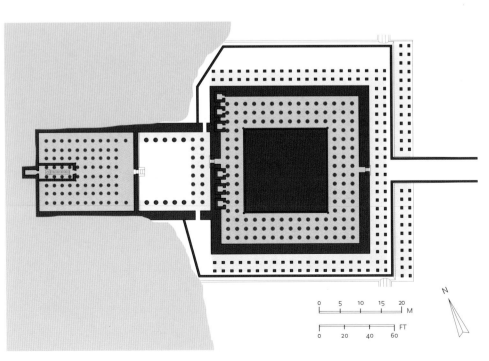

Plan of the mortuary temple of King Mentuhotep
It did not prove possible to extend the square-plan central part of the complex into a pyramid.

Temple precinct of the Middle Kingdom in Karnak
The oldest part of the Temple of Karnak, immediately in front of the banqueting-hall of Tuthmosis III has had no new structures built upon it for over 2000 years. However, practically all that remains of the temple constructed here in 2000 B.C. are door thresholds of granite and the base of a shrine for the cult image of Amun-Re.

all the blocks being later used in the construction of the Third Pylon of the Temple of Karnak during the reign of Amenhotep III (1390–1353 B.C.). In A.D. 1927–1938 the white limestone blocks that once made up this temple were excavated and put together again by Henri Chevrier in a complete reconstruction of the White Chapel. This is now on view in the open-air museum in Karnak. The roll moulding and the cavetto finishing of the top indicate that this kiosk was a stone version of a mud-brick structure; the low balustrades probably derive from the lightweight screens that used to be placed between the outer pillars of a kiosk. The reliefs encircling the building tone down the basic geometric shape of the square pillars. The graceful structure can be said in a way to rise out of the soil of the Nile valley, as its base is inscribed with the names of the districts of Upper and Lower Egypt, arranged in geographical order.

Despite recent finds of individual reliefs and architectural elements, the overall plan of the earliest temple complex of Karnak is still largely unknown. However, the significance of the shrine can at least be seen indirectly from the fact that as early as the end of Dynasty XI, in around 1991 B.C., a shrine had been erected towards Karnak on the Theban West bank: the little-known, small mud-brick temple of Mentuhotep III (2010–1990 B.C.), on the mountain of Toth high above the entrance to the Valley of the Kings. The entrance to this temple with its three sanctuaries is formed by a brick pylon, which is the earliest known example of this typical form of Egyptian temple gates.

The position of this small shrine, on a rather inaccessible mountain-top, indicates that there must have been many temples of the Middle Kingdom in Thebes. In a few places near Thebes, in Armant, Tod and Medamud, relief blocks with the names and representations of kings of Dynasties XI and XII have been found incorporated into later structures; the exceptionally high technical and stylistic quality of these reliefs

Page 81

Reliefs in the White Chapel in Karnak
The square pillars in the White Chapel, so called because of the white limestone used to build it, are decorated with flat reliefs depicting Sesostris I making a sacrifice to Amun-Re, the "King of the Gods". The striking relief pictures act as a counter to the strictly geometric structure of the building.
Middle Kingdom, Dynasty XII, c. 1950 B.C.

Head of a statue of King Sesostris I
Many architectural components and parts of statues from the oldest temple at Karnak have been found incorporated into later buildings. The statue head which was unearthed in front of the First Pylon of the Karnak Temple is one of a series of large pillar figures which probably once stood around a court. Their great size is an indication of the dimensions of the architecture that has been lost.
Middle Kingdom, Dynasty XII, c. 1950 B.C.; limestone; Luxor, Luxor Museum

The White Chapel of King Sesostris I in Karnak
Between 1927 and 1938 in the Temple of Karnak, a whole chapel was excavated block by block from the foundation walls of the Third Pylon, which was built by Amenhotep III (1390–1353 B.C.). 600 years earlier the chapel had been built as a staging shrine by Sesostris I for the jubilee celebrations for the renewal of kingship.
Middle Kingdom, Dynasty XII, c. 1950 B.C.

shows that Thebes retained its new role as the religious and artistic centre of the country, even after the royal court in the transition from Dynasty XI to XII moved north to Memphis in around 1991 B.C., the traditional site for the royal residence in the Old Kingdom. As a result of the move the terraced structure of tomb from Thebes, introduced by Mentuhotep II in Deir el-Bahari and continued nearby in the unfinished funerary complex of his successor, Mentuhotep III, was now replaced in Memphis by the traditional Old Kingdom shape of royal tomb, the pyramid.

Architectural aspirations in the Middle Kingdom were now directed towards building temples to the gods. The lack of such temples in the Old Kingdom is not solely explained by the fact that none have so far been discovered, but by the changed religious and political situation at the beginning of the Middle Kingdom. The individual districts in the kingdom had grown in significance and one way of expressing their new-found identity was through their local gods. Shrines were constructed throughout the land. Often they are only now to be found incorporated in the foundations of later buildings, but some individual parts of buildings have been discovered that afford us insight into the formal variety of architecture in this period of emergence.

One temple that was typical of many at the time was the Temple of Medinet Madi with its three sanctuaries; it was built at the end of Dynasty XII to the south-west of Cairo in the Fayum oasis, an area which was irrigated for cultivation during the Middle Kingdom. The Temple of Kasr el-Sagha, to the north of the Fayum, high on the edge of the desert, is an exception with its seven sanctuaries, and it appears all the more unusual because only the innermost temple section was actually completed, and the columned hall, court and pylon are lacking. No less original are the two shrines described by Herodotus – the monumental statues of Amenemhat III (1844–1797 B.C.) – of which all that now remains are their gigantic bases close to Medinet el-Fayum near Biahmu, and the unusual stela monument of the "Obelisk" of Abgig from the time of Sesostris I (1971–1926 B.C.).

Temple on the mountain of Toth in Western Thebes
Standing on one of the highest mountain peaks in Thebes is the small brick temple of Mentuhotep III. The pylon of this temple is an early example of a typically Egyptian form for temple entrances. The temple seems to be oriented towards Karnak on the opposite bank of the Nile.
Middle Kingdom, Dynasty XI, c. 2000 B.C.

Temple of Kasr el-Sagha in the Fayum

Nowadays this temple lies in the middle of a rocky desert in the Fayum oasis. Originally, however, the water level of the lake was much higher and the temple would have stood on the banks of the lake. The temple, consisting of seven sanctuaries arrayed in a line, was unfinished and there are no inscriptions indicating the names of the gods to whom it was to have been dedicated.
Middle Kingdom, Dynasty XII, c. 1800 B.C.

Temple gateway of Amenemhat II in Hermopolis

The remains of a large pylon in the centre of the temple ruins of Hermopolis indicate that this was once an important shrine in the Middle Kingdom, probably dedicated to the god Thoth or to the eight deities of Hermopolis.
Middle Kingdom, Dynasty XII, c. 1990 B.C.

Relief of Amenemhat I from Lisht
As in the Old Kingdom, the kings
of Dynasty XII also built pyramids.
Amenemhat I and Sesostris I chose
sites close to their residence in
Lisht. This relief, which was incorporated into another building,
probably comes from the completely destroyed mortuary
temple at Amenemhat's pyramid.
Middle Kingdom, Dynasty XII,
c. 1975 B.C.; limestone; New
York, The Metropolitan Museum
of Art

The joy of experimentation at the beginning of this new epoch is evident also in the architecture of the funerary complexes of Dynasty XII in Lisht, El-Lahun, Dahshour and Hawara. Their basic form is still derived from the pyramids of the Old Kingdom, but since the time of Sesostris II they consisted of millions of mud bricks, laid in layers and clad with limestone capping. In the system of corridors leading to the burial chamber, however, and in the temple complexes and enclosing walls, new forms and types of construction were being tried out, in the kind of innovative spirit reflected in the new depiction of man evident in the statues of the kings of Dynasty XII. The largest of the pyramid temples of the Middle Kingdom, built by Amenemhat III in Hawara on the eastern edge of the Fayum, is only preserved in descriptions by classical writers, who tell of this amazing "Labyrinth". The technical feats achieved in these pyramids reached gigantic proportions: the monolithic sarcophagus cham-ber in the Hawara pyramid weighs about 100 tons.

The remains of temples from the Middle Kingdom can only be seen in a few places, as most disappeared under new buildings or were cleared entirely. In Her-mopolis in Middle Egypt, a religious centre in Ancient Egypt, the remains of a temple gateway in limestone rise up in the middle of temple ruins from the New Kingdom, the Late and Ptolemaic Periods. Built by Amenemhat II in around 1900 B.C., the temple to which the gateway belongs must have been very large, and was probably dedicated to the god Thoth and the old gods of Hermopolis.

On the island of Elephantine, which since ancient times has marked the southern border of Egypt at the First Cataract on the Nile near today's Aswan, are the temples of Mentuhotep II and Sesostris I, the shrine for the local god Heqaib, and fortified walls dating back to the early Old Kingdom; all bear witness to a high level of building activity which reached far into the south, up to the Second Cataract, which became the new southern border of Egypt after the Nubian campaigns of the kings of Dynasty XII. In view of the military and political strength of Egypt's south-ern neighbour, the kingdom of Kerma, no fewer than fifteen forts were constructed in Lower Nubia and at the Second Cataract. Their associated tombs, bastions, gate-ways, drawbridges, rampart walks and embrasures are reminiscent of mediaeval fortresses, and in terms of their functionality and gigantic dimensions they are among the most impressive architectural achievements of the Middle Kingdom. Much excavation and documentation still remained to be done on these structures when they were flooded by Nasser's dam, but they are now lost to archaeological research for even.

Page 85 below
The fortress of Buhen
Expansion southwards to the
Second Cataract brought Egypt
into direct confrontation with the
Nubian kingdom of Kerma. Enormous fortresses were built to
secure the southern frontier. In
the course of construction of the
Aswan dam these buildings were
flooded and are now lost for ever.
Middle Kingdom, Dynasty XII,
c. 1900–1750 B.C.

Fortress of Buhen

The ditches, bastions and walls of these Middle Kingdom fortresses at the Second Cataract were a formidable obstacle to invasion by Egypt's southern neighbour, the Kingdom of Kerma. Small Egyptian towns grew up inside the fortress walls.

Middle Kingdom, Dynasty XII, c. 1900–1750 B.C.

The huge dimensions of these forts on the Second Cataract are to be understood primarily, but not exclusively, in terms of military and political considerations. These buildings also demonstrate the power of the Egyptian empire to those beyond. The inclusion of temple complexes in these fortresses also provides the border divine guardians. When, in the New Kingdom, King Sesostris III is depicted and named as the tutelary god of the Second Cataract in the Temple of Semna, this is evidence for the lasting effects of the architectural activities of the kings of the Middle Kingdom on the border with Upper Nubia.

On the Semna stele, found at the Second Cataract, Sesostris III himself comments on his presence at the border to the south: "I have pushed my border beyond that of my father, I have increased that which I inherited. Every son of mine who keeps this border that my majesty has made, he is my son. He that lets it fall and does not fight for it, he is not my son and was not born of me. My majesty has also had a statue of my majesty made on this border that my majesty has made, so that it will flourish and so that you will fight for it."

A similarly close link between architecture and royal cult at geopolitically extreme locations is to be found in the Sinai peninsula, in the eastern border region of Egypt. In Sarabit el-Khadim, in the middle of the turquoise mines area, kings of the Old and Middle Kingdoms appear as gods on reliefs and in inscriptions in a rock-cut temple of the Middle Kingdom and in the elongated asymmetrical front building of quite un-Egyptian design.

Semna stele of King Sesostris III
The long hieroglyphic text praises the Egyptian king as the glorious ruler of the world and describes the cowardice and weakness of his Nubian enemies. This piece of political propaganda originally stood near the Second Cataract. Middle Kingdom, Dynasty XII, c. 1820 B.C.; quartzite; Berlin, Ägyptisches Museum

Temple of Sarabit el-Khadim, Sinai
As far back as the Early Dynastic
Period and in the Old Kingdom the
Sinai peninsula was prized by the
Egyptians for its deposits of
turquoise and copper. The Temple
of Sarabit el-Khadim, which consists of a long series of courts
leading to an underground sanctuary, is one of the oldest examples of rock-cut temples in
Egyptian architecture.
Middle Kingdom, Dynasty XII,
c. 1800 B.C.

Despite the lack of any substantial archaeological remains of Middle Kingdom
temples to the gods in the Egyptian heartland, various indicators suggest that originally these temples were numerous. Building activities at the time are docu-
mented in authentic texts such as reports of royal building projects and Ancient
Egyptian architectural plans of temples. Fragmentary remains of a temple plan and
a hieratic text on the foundation of a temple by Sesostris I, for example, give an
impression of temple architecture in Heliopolis, one of the major religious centres
in Egypt; still the only existing visible remains of this temple at the site are the
obelisk of Sesostris I.

The Middle Kingdom is not a period of outstanding architectural achievement in
the history of Egypt, but it is one of the finest periods for sculpture. The portraits
of Dynasty XII are among the best Ancient Egyptian sculptural works and can take
their place alongside Greek and Roman likenesses. According to their inscriptions
the Middle Kingdom statues of kings and private people, mostly carved out of hard
stone, no longer served as tomb statues (as was their function in the third millennium), but were now placed in temples. Herein lies their exceptional significance for
architectural history, for as an inventory of the temples of the Middle Kingdom they
become indirect sources of information on their original locations, as we can read in
their inscriptions or deduced from their find places.

This produces names of regions of Egypt, which, for lack of any archaeological
remains, seem completely insignificant in architectural history. The Nile Delta to
the north of Cairo, one of the largest habitable expanses in Egypt, possesses only
limited traces of temples from the Middle Kingdom, in such places as Ezbet Rushdi,
Tell Ibrahim Awad and Bubastis. In Tanis, however, Egypt's capital city founded
around 1070 B.C. in the north-east of the Delta, many statues from the Middle Kingdom have been excavated. Before being dragged in around 1000 B.C. to decorate
the new metropolis in Tanis as 1 000-year-old monuments, these statues had stood
in the Delta residence of Ramesses II (1290–1224 B.C.), 30 km south of Tanis. Their

original locations were probably not far away, perhaps in Bubastis, near to the modern town of Zagazig in the east of the Delta. In Bubastis fragments of the colossal royal statues of Dynasty XII have been found, and it was here, too, that the ruins of a palace of King Amenemhet III have been excavated: surely one of the foremost of Egypt's centres of religion, rich in tradition.

The number and size of the statues of kings that were reused in Tanis is overwhelming. Ten seated figures of granite, each weighing about 8 to 10 tons, represent pharaohs from the early part of Dynasty XII. Two standing figures of Sesostris I, erected at the temple gates of Tanis, are almost 8 m high and among the largest of all Egyptian statues. The sphinx type is also present in Tanis in the form of two 5 m long granite sphinxes built under Amenemhet II and six monumental maned sphinxes from the time of Amenemhet III.

Analogous to the giant temple complexes of the New Kingdom in Thebes with their equally colossal statues, these recycled statues of rulers of the Middle Kingdom were probably also surrounded by gigantically proportioned sanctuaries. Sphinx avenues would have led up to towering pylons, the standing figures positioned either side of enormous gates, and seated statues erected between the pillars of broad temple courts.

Even in the case of the residence of the kings of the Middle Kingdom in Memphis, the impressive temple architecture of Dynasty XII can so far only be determined on the basis of indirect evidence. This evidence has been known for a long time, but not recognised as such: it comprises the colossal statues of the early part of Dynasty XII from the ruins of Memphis. Ramesses II had had their original inscriptions replaced with his own name, and so they were regarded as works typical of Ramesses' love of the gigantic until they were recently "unmasked" as statues from the Middle Kingdom.

Tomb of Khety in Beni Hasan
The roofs of the wide halls of the rock-cut tombs in Beni Hasan in Central Egypt are supported by slim lotus columns, which give the impression that the tomb is a canopy held up by plant columns. Middle Kingdom, Dynasty XI, c. 2000 B.C.

Tomb of Khnumhotep in Beni Hasan
Although the tombs of Beni Hasan are underground, rock-cut tombs, they also conform with the basic principle of Egyptian sacred architecture, whereby original wood and mud-brick forms are transposed into stone. Above the sixteen-cornered pillars at the entrance and the architrave we can see the stone versions of wooden beams used in roof construction. Middle Kingdom, Dynasty XII, c. 1900 B.C.

Thus the royal statues from Dynasty XII afford access to the architecture of that time and give it a status which can be compared with the finest products of the greatest period of Ancient Egyptian temple architecture, the New Kingdom and the Ptolemaic Period.

The non-royal architecture of the Middle Kingdom does not have to be tracked down through such convoluted routes, as it is preserved in several locations in impressive complexes. The district governors of the Middle Kingdom, who, alongside the central government in Memphis, exercised great political influence, had their cemeteries erected near to the district capitals. In the Nile valley in central and Upper Egypt these tombs are rock-cut. Often these subterranean tombs were located high up on a rocky outcrop in the mountains flanking the east and west sides of the Nile valley upriver between Cairo and Aswan. The choice of such an exposed position was determined by the search for layers of firm, solid rock that would give the best conditions for building stable structures and working the reliefs. A few of the rock-cut tombs are abandoned quarry caverns, for which the choice of site was also governed by the same criteria.

Some of these tombs, such as the ones in the Qan el-Kebir district, have the same elements as pyramid architecture – valley temple, corridor causeway and tomb chapel. In Beni Hasan in Middle Egypt, near to the capital of the Sixteenth Upper Egyptian nome, the tombs consist of a giant underground hall hewn out of an outcrop of rock. The columns are graceful clustered pillars with lotus capitals; they support architraves on which rests the barrel-vault-shaped roof, painted with textile patterns and mock wooden beams.

The large tomb halls at Beni Hasan, which can be seen as an autonomous new development in Egyptian architecture, thus follow the basic principle of religious architecture, in that they imitate the forms of secular architecture. The tomb hall is a monumental representation of a tent-like building with wooden poles hung with carpets. Forms taken from timber architecture are also visible in the tomb façades.

The extensive walls of these hall tombs in Beni Hasan show a wide-ranging pictorial programme carried out in painting. The motifs are taken almost exclusively from daily life, and in addition to the themes of handicraft, agriculture, hunting and games that derive from the tomb decoration of the Old Kingdom, they also contain compositions with many figures engaged in sieges and battles. Typical of these paintings in Beni Hasan are the wrestling scenes showing hundreds of pairs of wrestlers in the various stages of a wrestling match.

No less impressive than the hall tombs of Beni Hasan are the rock-cut tombs of the administrators of the southernmost of the Egyptian nomes near modern-day Aswan. The capital of the First Nome of Upper Egypt lay on the Nile island of Elephantine at the northern end of the First Cataract; the architectural history of this site from prehistoric times down to the Islamic period is piled up in a settlement hill some 15 m high. Shrines to the gods of the Cataracts area, the god of creation, Khnum, and the goddess Satet, date back to the Early Dynastic Period and include the temples of Mentuhotep II and Sesostris I, as well as a shrine for the local god, Heqaib, a deified nomarch governor of the Old Kingdom.

The tombs of the district administrators of Elephantine lie high up on the rocky desert slopes on the west bank of the Nile. Steep flights of steps lead directly up from the river's edge to a terrace-like, transverse outer court with portico, through which a columned hall is reached. A corridor leads deep into the mountainside to the cult chamber.

Rock-cut tombs in Aswan
All of the great necropolises of the Middle Kingdom have their own special architectural features. The local governors of Elephantine, who had grown rich through controlling the trade with the south, were buried high on the edge of the desert on the west bank of the Nile. Their tombs were cut into the rock, and each had an outer court with steep steps leading down to the river.
Middle Kingdom, Dynasty XII, 1900–1800 B.C.

Pectoral of King Sesostris III
The programmatic motif of this chest decoration showing the king as a griffon above his enemies is placed in an architectural context. Lotus columns and cavetto indicate a temple building, on the roof of which the vulture, as a protecting deity, spreads out its wings. Middle Kingdom, Dynasty XII, c. 1820 B.C.; gold, carnelian, lapis lazuli; Cairo, Egyptian Museum

Each of the rock necropolises of the Middle Kingdom displays local peculiarities in its style of architecture, relief carving and painting. Wide, pillared façades are typical of Thebes, for example, whereas statue shrines in front of the back wall of the cult room are only found in Meir, and in Assiut the forms and dimensions of the rock-cut graves of the nomarchs seem to anticipate the rock temples of the New Kingdom.

Finally, some of the most precious and artistically valuable examples of architecture in the Middle Kingdom are the items of jewellery either formed to look like miniature temples, or containing iconographic references to them. Typical Middle Kingdom pectorals show the form of a temple façade with banked walls, roll moulding and cavetto. In concentrated form these items bear witness to the claim of the Middle Kingdom to be the classical period of Ancient Egypt, not only with respect to the fine arts, literature and writing, but also to architecture.

A State Built of Stone

Temples to the Gods in the New Kingdom

Page 93
**Head of a statue of King
Tuthmosis III**
Tuthmosis III was one of the keen-
est builders in the entire three-
thousand years of Egyptian history. He had temples built in all
the important places in his empire,
from the Nile delta to Gebel
Barkal in the Sudan.
New Kingdom, Dynasty XVIII,
c. 1450 B.C.; greywacke; Luxor,
Luxor Museum

Statue shrine
The temple as an earthly home of
the gods was the most important
aim of architecture in Egypt. This
repoussé-work statue shrine in
gold leaf is a miniature model of a
god's house. It was found in the
tomb of Tutankhamun. The sloping walls, cavetto and roof arching
towards the front are an imitation
of features found in the oldest
type of brick architecture and
tent-roofed shelters.
New Kingdom, Dynasty XVIII,
c. 1325 B.C.; wood and gold leaf;
Cairo, Egyptian Museum

The Temple City of Karnak and Luxor

The physical presence of the ancient world is perhaps nowhere so immediately felt as in the temple city of Karnak. Still today, as if it were a living shrine, visitors are drawn into its spell and hushed into silence, surrounded by the sacred aura of another world.

The origins of Karnak lay at the beginning of the Middle Kingdom, around 2000 B.C., when for a short time Thebes became the capital of Egypt; the Temple of Amun-Re, built in this period, soon rose to become the most important shrine in the whole of Egypt. Every pharaoh saw it as his religious and political duty to extend it and to add to its splendour. From the Middle Kingdom onwards to make private donations of statues to be placed in the court of the Amun temple was a popular religious practice; those who in this way were close to the temple lord, Amun-Re, were ensured of his help and grace. Over the centuries thousands of votive figures, small bronze statuettes and giant-sized granite figures were donated to Karnak. Many of them were rediscovered in pits in which they had been thrown during the periodic "tidying up" of the temple.

Despite the almost 2 000 years of architectural history at Karnak the temple's ground plan is still clear and legible. A main axis runs from the inner Sanctuary in the east towards the Nile in the west, corresponding to the traditional orientation of Ancient Egyptian temples, which were placed at right angles to the theoretical south-north axis of the course of the Nile. A second axis branches off the first, from north to south, and the extension of this leads to an independent temple complex dedicated to the goddess Mut, the consort of Amun-Re.

Along these coordinates are arranged the temple gateways or pylons, in not always exact chronological order from the inside to the outside. In front of these pylons with their two towers with slanting walls stood colossal statues, flagpoles and obelisks. What we see today as a temple structure is actually just a sequence of portals leading to a central zone which has been the earthly home of the gods since the temple was founded in the early Middle Kingdom.

Between the pylons of the east-west axis pillared halls were built, which turned the original open courts into closed temple rooms.

The Hypostyle Hall of Karnak with its 134 columns and a floor area of 5 500 m^2 is the largest enclosed space in Egyptian architecture and is a representative example of such a hall. Under Amenhotep III (1390–1353 B.C.) the Third Pylon formed the west façade of the temple of Amun. Under Amenhotep IV (Akhenaten) (1353–1336 B.C.) building work stopped on the shrine of Amun-Re, who had to give way to the monotheistic god Aten. In about 1320 B.C., Horemheb, the last ruler of Dynasty XVIII, moved the temple façade further west by building the Second Pylon. At the beginning of Dynasty XIX under Sethos I and Ramesses II the two temple gates were linked together by means of a double row of 21-m high columns with opened papyrus capitals; this gave rise to three raised central aisles, which were flanked by seven side aisles with low roofs supported on papyrus columns with closed capitals.

Sphinx avenue in front of the Temple of Karnak

The divine inhabitant of the temple remains hidden in the form of a cult image within the innermost sanctuary of the temple. In front of the temple the god shows himself in a variety of statue forms. Sphinxes were used to flank temple portals since the days of the Old Kingdom. The sphinxes either side of the main approach to the Temple of Karnak have a lion's body and the ram's head of Amun.
New Kingdom, Dynasty XVIII, c. 1380 B.C.; sandstone

Page 97

Ram-headed sphinx in the Temple of Amun in Karnak

A statue of the king stands between the lion's paws and under the ram's head of the sphinx figure of the god of Amun. The king is portrayed as a god-like being, in the form of Khonsu.
New Kingdom, Dynasty XIX, c. 1250 B.C.

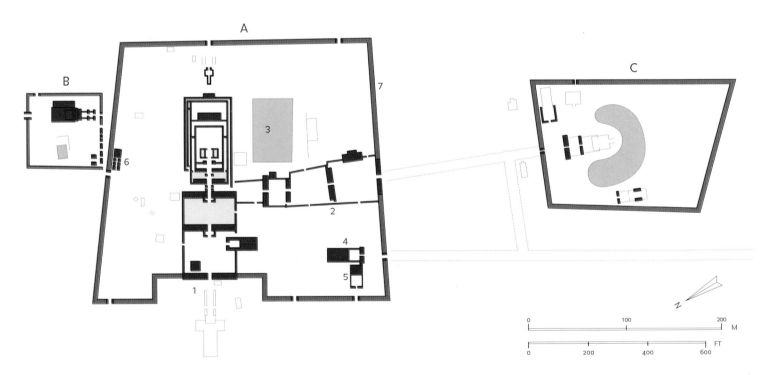

General plan of Karnak
Two southern axes lead off the
main east-west axis of the Temple
of Amun. They are oriented towards the Temple of Mut and to
Luxor.

A Amun complex
  1. Main building of the Temple
    of Amun
  2. Secondary axis of the Tem-
    ple of Amun
  3. Holy lake

4. Temple of Khonsu
5. Temple of Ipet
6. Temple of Ptah
7. Circumference wall
B Montu complex
C Mut complex

Page 98 above
Reconstruction of the temple city of Karnak

Intensive archaeological research has enabled us to piece together how this unique conglomeration of sacred buildings would originally have looked. The complex ranges from the Temple of Montu in the north, via the extensive Temple of Amun, through to the Temple of the goddess Mut in the south.

The Hypostyle Hall in the Temple of Amun in Karnak

134 columns stand in the Hypostyle Hall of the Temple of Amun, in a wide courtyard between the Second and the Third Pylons. As stone imitations of plant columns and with widely opened papyrus capitals they give an appearance of lightness, belying their great weight.
New Kingdom, Dynasty XIX, c. 1290–1250 B.C.

The spatial impression thus created is not one of a closed, compact building volume, but of a covered courtyard with the emphasis on the central aisle. Yet despite the enormous dimensions of its components the Hypostyle Hall of Karnak does not appear as an oppressive stone structure, but maintains instead a certain clear elegance. The lightness of the plant columns, still recognisable as a monumental representation of naturalistic forms, the tapering of the shafts and the papyrus capitals all conjure up the image of a papyrus thicket, with the sky vaulting above. An extension in front of the Second Pylon takes up this idea and develops it in the kiosk of King Taharqa (690–664 B.C.) in which papyrus columns rise up under an open sky as if they were some kind of interpretative aid to understanding the hypostyle hall.

Not until the Ptolemaic Period did the architectural history of the Temple of Amun reach its close with the construction of the First Pylon, which at 100 m wide, was to be the largest temple gate in Egypt. However, it was never completed; its sandstone blocks are still at the bossage stage, the crowning cavetto was never mounted and in several places even today we can still see the construction ramps made of unfired bricks. These ramps were to be used to transport the sandstone blocks of the Pylon to their originally planned height of 34 m.

The cult activities in this, the largest and most significant shrine in Egypt, can still be deduced today from many architectural details. In front of the First Pylon is a small harbour basin with a canal link to the Nile. This was the mooring place for the god's barque aboard which Amun-Re sailed in ceremonial procession to the Temple of Luxor and to the Theban temples on the west bank of the Nile opposite Karnak. An avenue of monumental sandstone rams, the holy animals of Amun, leads to the temple entrance. On both sides of this path of the gods, in front of the temple gates

of the Second Pylon, are the small temples of Sethos II (1214–1204 B.C.) and Ramesses III (1194–1163 B.C.), whose cultic centre consists of three shrines next to each other, chapels for the images of the Holy Family of Karnak, the gods Amun-Re and Mut and their son, Khonsu.

The royal patrons of these "repository temples" thus provide a resting place for the divine triad of Karnak, a place which they could enter during the procession and from where they could respond to the devotion regularly shown to them by the pharaoh, in daily sacrifices and in the regular festivals for the gods held throughout the year.

Behind the hypostyle hall and the closely positioned Pylons III to VI there is the first cult focus, the chamber for the sacred barque, so called because of its function as the place for the barque in which the divine image was placed for the procession. The granite sanctuary occupying this central place in Karnak was built in about 320 B.C. by Philip Arrhidaeus, the successor of Alexander the Great; it stands on the spot where, more than a thousand years before, Queen Hatshepsut had built a sanctuary of red quartzite, the "Chapelle Rouge". This chapel, however, soon had to give way to a new building, constructed under Tuthmosis III, but fortunately a large part of this older chapel still remains, thanks to the habit of Ancient Egyptian builders of "recycling" components from demolished structures. More than 300 blocks, two-thirds of the entire chapel building, were rediscovered in the foundations of the Third Pylon, where they had been put in the time of Amenhotep III.

The precisely cut, hollow reliefs on this chapel are a pictorial record of the cult activities in the Temple of Amun-Re and also a unique masterpiece of the relief art of the New Kingdom.

The axial approach from the First to the Sixth Pylon ends here; from here the procession of the divine image takes a circuitous route to the inner sanctuary. It proceeds around the venerable "Court of the Middle Kingdom" and through Tuthmosis III's festival hall, which is at right angles to the temple axis; this part of the temple is also a kind of stone court, with lightweight columns shaped like tent poles supporting a sun-shading roof.

Behind the festival hall of Tuthmosis III, in a rather inaccessible place, is the inner sanctuary. The huge block of red granite on which the shrine of the golden cult statue of Amun-Re, the "King of the gods", stood, is still today preserved in its original position. Immediately in front of the inner sanctuary are two rooms, whose current description as "Botanical Gardens" conjures up false associations. The wall reliefs in these temple rooms, created under Tuthmosis III, depict in great detail the

Page 101

Temple of Amun in Karnak
Nowadays we can look straight down the central axis of the Temple of Amun to the sanctuary for the divine barque, but once massive doors with metal hinges formed a barrier between the pylons, marking a clear division between the sacred and the secular worlds.
Second Pylon with the kiosk of King Taharka in front; New Kingdom, Dynasty XVIII, c. 1300 B.C., and Late Period, Dynasty XXV, c. 680 B.C.

Relief picture on the Third Pylon of Karnak
Once a year, for the great Feast of Opet, Amun travelled from Karnak to Luxor, with his wife, Mut and son, Khonsu. A relief cycle in Luxor indicates the route of the procession and shows the temple façade at the time of Tutankhamun and the Third Pylon complete with flagpoles.
New Kingdom, Dynasty XVIII, c. 1330 B.C.

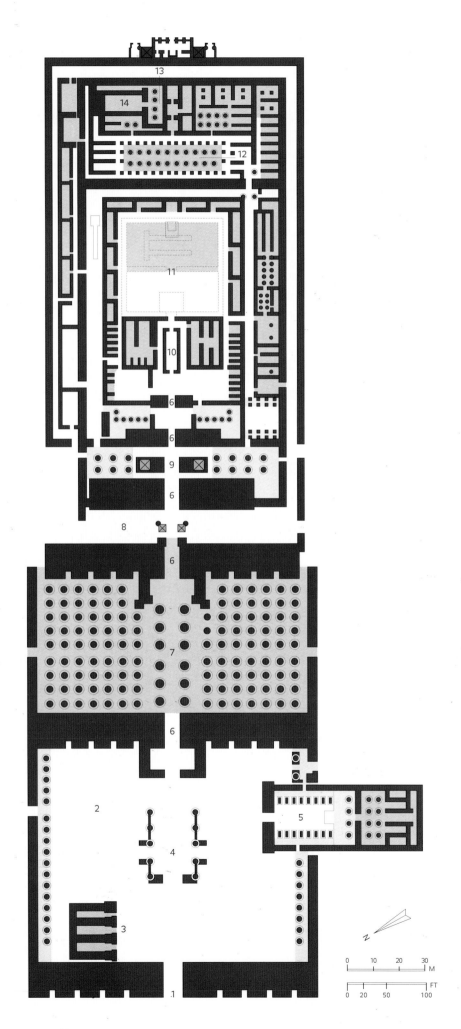

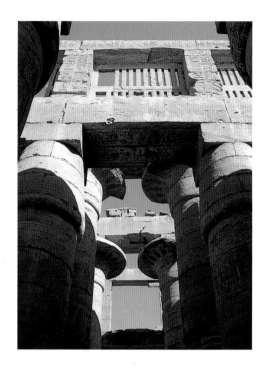

Hypostyle Hall in the Temple of Amun in Karnak
Window grilles, integrated in the walls, bridged the height difference between the central and side aisles and let in the only light source to the enormous hall. New Kingdom, Dynasty XIX, c. 1290–1250 B.C.

Page 103
Hypostyle Hall in the Temple of Amun in Karnak
The reliefs on the columns indicate the route taken by the processions. New Kingdom, Dynasty XIX, c. 1290–1250 B.C.

Plan of the Temple of Amun
From the Middle Kingdom precinct (c. 2000 B.C.), the Temple of Amun was extended outwards over a period of 2000 years as far as the unfinished First Pylon. The courts between the Second and Third Pylons and between the Fourth and Fifth Pylons were built as columned halls.
1. Pylon I, 2. Court, 3. Temple of Sethos II, 4. Kiosk of Taharka, 5. Temple of Ramesses III, 6. Pylons II–VI, 7. Hypostyle Hall, 8. Obelisks of Tuthmosis I, 9. Obelisks of Hatshepsut, 10. Sanctuary of the barque, 11. "Court" of the Middle Kingdom, 12. Festival Hall of Tuthmosis III, 13. "Botanical Garden", 14. Inner Sanctuary

Temple of Ramesses III in Karnak
In front of the temple a number of kings erected staging temples where the cult images of the divine family paused when leaving the temple. It was the divine duty of the kings to continue the expansion of the temple.
New Kingdom, Dynasty XX, c. 1180–1160 B.C.

animal and plant world of Egypt and its neighbours, in the form of a pictorial encyclopaedia of zoology and botany. The meaning behind these unusual pictures lies in the presentation of the work of creation of the "King of the gods", Amun-Re. Their theological function corresponds to that of the season reliefs of Nyuserre in the sun temple of Abu Ghurab, and to the reliefs of the sun temple of Akhenaten in Amarna.

In the east, outside the Temple of Amun and the wall surrounding it, is a small sanctuary in which Amun-Re was worshipped at a 32-m high obelisk, now standing in Rome in front of the basilica of Saint John of Lateran. In this part of Karnak Amun-Re was honoured as "Amun, who hears the prayers", this role of a popular divinity being echoed also in a shrine to the south of the Temple of Amun begun by Ramesses III and dedicated to the god Khonsu. "Khonsu, the Advice-Giver" was revered as a god not only in Egypt but also far beyond its borders. In the sequence of gateway,

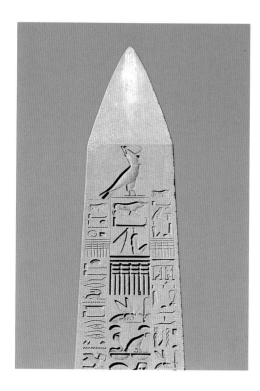

Obelisk of Tuthmosis I in Karnak
In front of the temple gate, or
pylon, stood pairs of obelisks with
golden tips which reflected the
first and last rays of the sun each
day – a symbolic image of the
presence of the sun god on earth
and of his daily cycle.
New Kingdom, Dynasty XVIII,
c. 1490 B.C.

Obelisk of Hatshepsut in Karnak
The obelisks of Karnak once stood
in front of the temple, but later
building work around them effect-
ively placed them inside the
temple complex, away from view.
New Kingdom, Dynasty XVIII,
c. 1470 B.C.

Relief of Hatshepsut
On one of the quartzite blocks in
the "Chapelle Rouge" Queen Hatshepsut is shown dedicating to the
god Amun "two great obelisks,
covered with white gold, and so
high that they pierce the skies".
New Kingdom, Dynasty XVIII,
c. 1470 B.C.; Luxor, Luxor
Museum

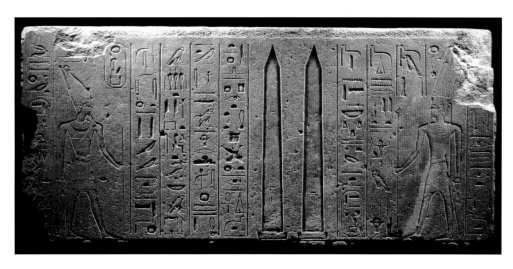

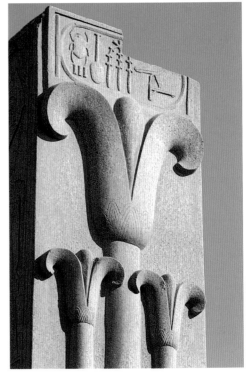

Pillar in front of the sanctuary of the divine barque in Karnak

The plant symbols of Upper and Lower Egypt, the lily and the papyrus, are supported by a square, free-standing pillar erected in the centre of the Temple of Amun, in front of the sanctuary where the divine barque was stored. The roof they support is the open sky. The architecture of the temple is thus directly linked with the cosmos. New Kingdom, Dynasty XVIII, c. 1450 B.C.

Side view of the symbolic pillar of Upper Egypt in Karnak

Mut, the divine wife of Amun, embraces King Tuthmosis III. The emblematic sparseness of the plant and cartouche motif becomes an image for the physical encounter between king and goddess. New Kingdom, Dynasty XVIII, c. 1450 B.C.

Symbolic pillar of Upper Egypt in the Temple of Amun

At the top of the pillar, where the earth meets the sky, and above the three lilies which are the symbol of Upper Egypt, is a cartouche bearing the name of Tuthmosis III. The imagery for the role of the king as an intermediary between god and man is thus clear.
New Kingdom, Dynasty XVIII, c. 1450 B.C.

sphinx avenue, kiosk, pylon, court, columned hall, barque sanctuary, anteroom and inner sanctuary, the Temple of Khonsu is a classic example of a New Kingdom temple to the gods. An avenue bordered by statues of rams leads from this temple for a distance of 2.5 kilometres to the south to the Temple of Luxor, which forms a cult unit with the Amun complex.

To the east, beyond the outer brick wall enclosing the whole Amun complex, Amenhotep IV had a sun temple built in honour of Aten. This was in about 1353 B.C. at the beginning of the king's religious reforms, and the temple plan is a forerunner of the later temple architecture of Amarna. The remains of about forty colossal statues of the king have been recovered on the site, and over 40 000 blocks with reliefs from the temple walls have been found re-used in the Ninth Pylon, built at the end of Dynasty XVIII under King Horemheb.

As large as the temple complex of Amun-Re at Karnak may seem, it is itself but part of an even larger ensemble. To the north of the complex is the Temple of Montu, in the south-east, the Temple of Mut, and further south, close to the Nile, the Temple of Luxor, known in Ancient Egypt as the Opet, meaning "the harem".

Procession of the divine barque

The procession of the cult image of Amun is depicted on a block in the "Chapelle Rouge". Hidden in an enclosed shrine on the divine barque, recognisable by the ram's head decoration on stern and bow, the cult image is carried out of the temple by priests.
New Kingdom, Dynasty XVIII, c. 1470 B.C.

This is where Amun-Re celebrated his divine marriage, once a year, following a noisy procession on the Nile from Karnak to Luxor. At the end of the festival the procession filed down the sphinx avenue back to Karnak.

The temple façade we see today, facing north in the direction of Karnak, is dominated by the pylon erected by Ramesses II. Four colossal standing figures and two seated figures of the king, and two obelisks and four flag masts form a classical temple front, backed by a giant relief cycle of the Battle of Kadesh, worked in sunken relief on the pylon façade. In the court behind the pylon stand colossal granite statues of Ramesses II, placed between the columns of the double-row perimeter colonnade, and two monumental seated figures flank the gateway to the

Page 109 above
"Botanical Garden" in Karnak
This popular name for one of the innermost rooms in the Temple of Amun gives a false impression. The room has four papyrus-bundle columns and on the walls are detailed pictures of animals and plants, which have given rise to its current name.
New Kingdom, Dynasty XVIII, c. 1450 B.C.

Festival hall of Tuthmosis III in Karnak
As in the case of so many Egyptian temple rooms the festival hall of Tuthmosis III is not in fact an enclosed space, but a courtyard in which are placed free-standing columns which support a stone representation of a light canopy as a shade from the sun. This function of the columns explains their unusual form, which imitates tent poles.
New Kingdom, Dynasty XVIII, c. 1450 B.C.

Relief in the "Botanical Garden"
The animals and plants depicted in the reliefs are not shown in their natural surroundings, but in a kind of reference work which is a pictorial homage to the god Amun, who is manifested on earth through his creations.
New Kingdom, Dynasty XVIII, c. 1450 B.C.

The holy lake at the **Temple of Amun in Karnak**
This modern reconstruction of the lake corresponds to what it originally looked like. The holy lake was not only a reservoir of water, but also an image of the primeval ocean and a stage for cult rituals. It was also a fixed component of an Egyptian temple.

Obelisk of Hatshepsut in Karnak
The Horus falcon wearing the crown of Upper and Lower Egypt represents the divinity of the king. It is seen here placed above the first of the five names of the ruler, the other names reading vertically on the shaft of the obelisk. New Kingdom, Dynasty XVIII, c. 1450 B.C.

Temple of the god Khonsu in Karnak

Also part of the temple complex of Karnak is a temple to the goddess Mut and a separate shrine to the god Khonsu, the son of Amun and Mut. The slits in the façade of the pylon are for fixing flagpoles.
New Kingdom, Dynasty XX, c. 1180–1160 B.C.

Columned hall of the Temple of Khonsu

The well preserved Temple of Khonsu gives an authentic impression of the atmosphere in temples. The sequence of spaces progresses from the court, through the columned hall and into the innermost sanctuary.
New Kingdom, Dynasty XX, c. 1180–1160 B.C.

Façade of the Temple of Luxor
With the obelisks and colossal seated and standing statues the Temple of Luxor retains part of the original elements of an Ancient Egyptian temple façade. The picture reliefs on the pylon walls, which tell the story of Ramesses III's Battle of Kadesh, were painted and thus very prominent. New Kingdom, Dynasty XIX, c. 1280–1220 B.C.

Relief picture in the Temple of Luxor
Depicted in a relief in the first court of the Temple of Luxor is the temple façade as it looked in the time of Ramesses II. In front of the right-hand pylon tower we can see an obelisk and two flagpoles, as well as two standing figures. This detailed relief has made it possible to reconstruct a picture of how the area in front of the temple looked, particularly as many of the original pieces have survived. New Kingdom, Dynasty XIX, c. 1250 B.C.

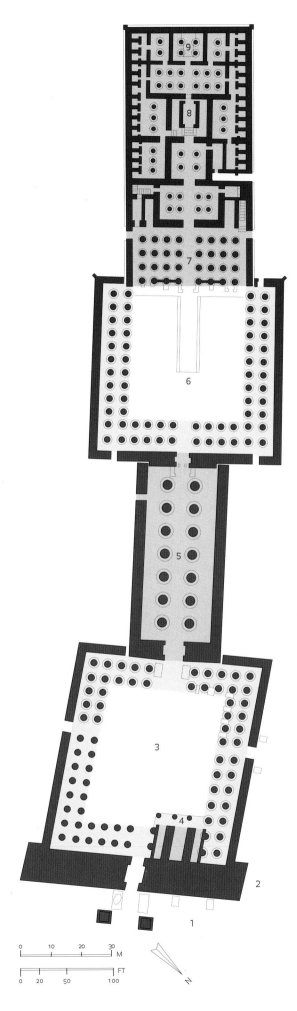

Plan of the Temple of Luxor

Ramesses II only built the pylon and the first court. A change in the direction of the axis indicates their later construction. The colonnade, second court, columned hall and innermost temple rooms were built in the time of Amenhotep III as the "harem" of Amun. This was the place to which Amun came from Karnak once a year to celebrate his divine marriage.

1. Outer court with obelisks and colossal statues
2. Pylon
3. Court of Ramesses III
4. Temple of Tuthmosis III
5. Colonnade of Amenophis III
6. Court of Amenophis III
7. Columned hall
8. Sanctuary of the barque
9. Inner sanctuary

The Obelisk of Luxor in Paris

The western obelisk which originally stood in front of the Temple of Luxor was given to the French as a present by Viceroy Muhammed Ali. In its position at the centre of the Place de la Concorde, it has now become a symbol of the French capital, even rivalling the Eiffel Tower. New Kingdom, Dynasty XIX, c. 1250 B.C.

The Lateran Obelisk from Karnak in Rome

Ancient Egyptian antiquities have not only been shipped to Europe in recent times. Roman emperors also liked to bring Egyptian monuments back to Rome, either as trophies from the conquered land around the Nile, or as a historic and religiously symbolic item with which to decorate the temples to Egyptian gods in Rome. The obelisk in front of the Lateran basilica in Rome originally stood in the eastern part of the Temple of Amun in Karnak. The Emperor Augustus had it brought to Rome and placed in the Circus Maximus. New Kingdom, Dynasty XVIII, c. 1400 B.C.

pillared walkway. The walkway walls, either side of the 21-m high papyrus columns, are decorated with a relief cycle vividly depicting the festival procession between Karnak and Luxor. These reliefs were worked under Tutankhamun, in about 1325 B.C., but still show strong influences from the style common under Akhenaten and Nefertiti.

Behind this colonnade is the court of Amenhotep III, which is one of the most beautiful spaces in Ancient Egyptian architecture; here, in true Ancient Egyptian tradition, no distinction is made between the heavens and their representation in the context of the temple. The papyrus-bundle columns around the court and the pronaos immediately adjacent to the court tower up to the sky, turning the heavens into the roof over the space and making this man-made temple into a part of the cosmos.

Statues of gods and kings found in this court just a few years ago date from Dynasty XVIII through to the Late Period and indicate that the Temple of Luxor was an important centre of cult worship. As a mythological place the Temple of Luxor is the place within the theological structure of the temples of Thebes in which king and god-king, in other words the pharaoh and Amun-Re, came into immediate contact with each other. Reliefs in the Luxor temple show the divine origins of King Amenhotep III. The earthly mother of the king is made pregnant by the king of gods Amun-Re; the king is the son of god and yet also a human being – the analogy here

Colossal statue of Ramesses II in Luxor
The court of Ramesses II in the Temple of Luxor is ringed with statues, some of which date from the time of Amenhotep III; others were created under Ramesses II as part of an extension of the temple complex. The seated figure shows Ramesses II as a divine king, here given the additional name of "Sun of the Rulers".
New Kingdom, Dynasty XIX, c. 1250 B.C.

with the birth of Christ in the New Testament is clear. Luxor is the birth-house of the Temple of Karnak; it is the place where god comes to earth and the human king becomes divine.

The ideology of the divinity of the king and the closeness of god to humanity is ritually expressed in the Feast of Opet, in the marriage feast of Amun-Re, which was celebrated not in holy seclusion, but right in the middle of the bustling capital city, for Karnak and Luxor were in the centre of Thebes, like mediaeval cathedrals. Similarly the temples were an integral part of the political and economic life of the metropolises; the land owned by these temples and the tax-collecting functions of the temple authorities represented a not inconsiderable political power which could quite conceivably also have been used against the state authorities and the royal house.

Page 117
Second Court of the Temple of Luxor
The broad court of Amenhotep III in the Temple of Luxor is surrounded by bundle columns with closed papyrus capitals. The architraves support the sky as a roof, which heightens the impression of the court as the symbiosis of architecture and cosmos. Under the wide expanse of the skies, the natural models re-emerge from the stone columns.
New Kingdom, Dynasty XVIII, c. 1370 B.C.

Colonnade of Amenhotep III in the Temple of Luxor

An enormous colonnade was placed in front of the temple of Amenhotep III in Luxor. The papyrus columns are built of individual, drum-shaped sandstone blocks. Along the side walls is a long relief cycle from the time of Tutankhamun, showing the annual Feast of Opet.
New Kingdom, Dynasty XVIII, c. 1360 B.C.

Thebes in Ancient Egypt

The complex of the Temple of Karnak in the north and the Temple of Luxor in the south were the cornerstones of "Thebes of a hundred gateways". The main axis of the city was formed by a processional street, more than 2 km long and lined with statues of sphinxes. The street linked the two temples. Thebes was the religious centre of Egypt for 2 000 years.

Sun Temple of Amenhotep IV in Karnak (Impression)

Tens of thousands of relief blocks from the time of Amenhotep IV have been excavated in Luxor and Karnak, where they were re-used in the foundations and as additional material for later buildings. Originally they belonged to temples to the sun god, Aten, built by Amenhotep IV at the beginning of his reign. At the end of Dynasty XVIII, in the reign of Horemheb, these temples were destroyed with the aim of eradicating the epoch of the "traitor king" from history. Through a systematic investigation of these blocks it is possible to reconstruct the picture sequences and the original architectural form of the open courts with their free-standing pillars.

Amarna

When, in around 1350 B.C., Thebes lost its unchallenged position as spiritual centre of the country, it was probably just this amalgamation of religion and politics, of cult and commerce that prompted King Amenhotep IV to initiate a religious revolution of quite enormous consequences for the future, even if it was not consistently followed in Egypt.

With the abandonment of the holy family of Amun-Re, Mut and Khonsu, and all the other various sacred forms and names of god that had established themselves over the course of one and a half millennia, Amenhotep IV cleared the way for a single god, called the Aten, meaning "the sun", a god that could be depicted in only one way, as the sun disk high in the sky, sending out its rays to earth in the form of outstretched human hands.

An appropriate architectural form had to be found for this new monotheistic world-view. The Aten, the god of the sun, lived in the heavens. His places of veneration were broad courts, open to the skies. This type of temple had already been prefigured in the Temple of Amenhotep III in Luxor, and as such was not a new style, as the court had always been an important element in the basic language of Egyptian temple architecture, as a place where earth and sky, god and man met. The first of these sun temples to the Aten was built in Karnak shortly after Amenhotep IV came to power (around 1353 B.C.), on a site close to and in confrontation with the Temple of Amun-Re. The remains of a large court to the east of the Temple of Amun have been excavated and colossal standing figures in sandstone have been found, depicting the king as the earthly representation of the god of creation and giving him almost female body forms.

Painted floor from Amarna

A main theme in art during the Amarna period was the depiction of life in nature, as an immediate expression of the presence of the sun god Aten on earth. The impressionistic pictures of nature painted on the floors of the royal palaces created a scene like a papyrus jungle. "The birds have flown their nests, their wings praise your ka", are the words in the great sun song of the king. New Kingdom, Dynasty XVIII, c. 1348–1335 B.C.; painting on stucco; Berlin, Ägyptisches Museum

Five years after coming to power the king and his entire court moved from the capital city of Thebes to Egypt's new metropolis, Amarna (the modern name). Originally called Akhetaten, the "light place of the Aten", this was a new town, straight from the drawing-board, built half-way between Thebes and Memphis. The king took the name of Akhenaten, meaning "well-pleasing to the Aten", and the boundary stelae around Amarna are inscribed with his royal decree concerning the foundation of the town: "The Aten, my father, it was that pointed to Akhetaten. Look, the pharaoh found it! No god, no goddess, no ruler, no official and no person can lay claim to it. I erect Akhetaten for the Aten, my father, at this place. I build the great temple for the Aten, my father, in Akhetaten in this place. And I build the small temple for the Aten, my father, in Akhetaten in this place. I build the sun-shadow chapel for the great royal consort Nefertiti of the Aten, my father, in Akhetaten in this place. I build a jubilee temple for the Aten, my father, on the island of the Aten in Akhetaten in this place [...]. I build for myself palaces for the pharaoh, and I build a harem for the royal consort in Akhetaten in this place. I have a tomb built in the mountain of Akhetaten, where the sun rises, where I shall be buried after the millions of year's reign, that the Aten, my father, has allocated to me [...]. Tomb complexes are built for the high priests and for the heavenly fathers of the Aten and for the servants of the Aten in the mountain of Akhetaten, where the sun rises [...]."

A century of archaeological excavation in Amarna has brought the foundation walls of this new royal capital city of Egypt to light again. We can now see the remains of the large temple with its sequence of open courts in which hundreds of sacrificial altars stood, the Small Temple and the palaces lining the processional route which runs from north to south through the entire town for a distance of about 5 km.

Relief block from Amarna

Blocks from palaces and temples in Amarna which were re-used in Hermopolis give exact information about the city of Akhenaten. An overall picture of the architecture in Amarna can be built up using information found on reliefs on these blocks and from excavations of the ground plans of buildings in Amarna. This relief block shows a part of the royal palace with the window of appearances.
New Kingdom, Dynasty XVIII, c. 1348–1335 B.C.; limestone; Boston, Museum of Fine Arts

General plan of Amarna

The city of Amarna, covering several kilometres, was built within the space of a few years on the edge of the desert, not far from the Nile. After just one-and-a-half decades the city was abandoned. The royal palace and temples are situated in the centre of the city, on both sides of the Royal Road.

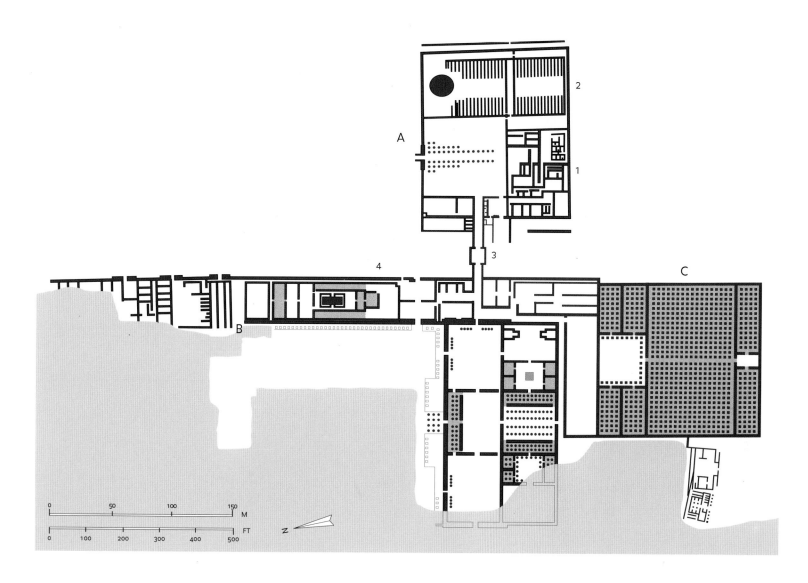

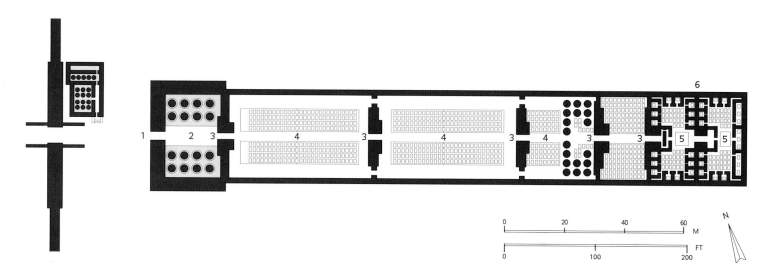

The palace district in Amarna
The Palace of the King lies on both sides of the Royal Road. The private and official parts of the building were linked by a bridge. The royal couple showed themselves to the people from this bridge.

A Palace residence
  1. King's residence
  2. Store rooms
  3. Bridge
  4. "Royal Road"
B "Harem"
C Official palace

The Great Temple of Aten
Aten, the sun god, lives in the skies. His temples incorporate the skies in their architectural concept, by replacing closed spaces with open courts. Hundreds of altars, placed close together in these courts, were used for making sacrifices to the Aten under the open skies.

1. Pylon I
2. Ceremonial hall
3. Pylons II–VI
4. Courts with altars
5. Altars
6. Courts with chapels

In the centre of the town a walled bridge with three openings spanned the processional route and linked two palace buildings. The royal couple gave their audiences from the window of appearances in the middle of the bridge. In the south of the town extended the districts with villas and workshops, divided into noble streets and more modest areas. The rock-cut graves are high up on the cliffs which form a semicircle to the east of the city. Far away to the east of the town is the king's tomb, in a lonely desert valley, after the example of the Theban royal tombs.

No other place in Egypt gives us so much insight into ancient town planning as Amarna. Although at the end of Dynasty XVIII Akhenaten's successors razed the temples and palaces to the ground, leaving only the foundation walls (the same fate befell the Temple of Aten in Karnak), this ancient city can nevertheless still be authentically reconstructed, thanks to the very detailed relief pictures in the tombs of Amarna which give precise information on the town. Further relief images of the town are to be found on the limestone blocks which originally formed the temple walls. Under Ramesses II the walls were dismantled and the blocks re-used in nearby Hermopolis as building material for a temple, ensuring their survival.

As the town was only inhabited for about fifteen years, many of the secular buildings, which unlike the temples of Aten were not destroyed, have survived well, even down to parts of the wall paintings and interior fittings. The most spectacular find is undoubtedly the studio of the court sculptor of Akhetaten, where many portrait studies in plaster were discovered, as well as the world-famous bust of Nefertari. The excavations in Amarna continue each year and are now bringing to light some of the houses and workshops of ordinary workers on the edge of town. This "Horizon of the Aten" is thus increasing in significance for settlement archaeology and for the social history of Egypt, those more difficult areas that have always been robbed of the limelight by the more spectacular temples and tombs.

Relief picture of a temple of Aten
The architectural concept of opening up towards the skies is also seen in the construction of doors and gateways. Depictions of architecture in temple reliefs from Amarna show that in the temples of Aten open architraves had replaced closed door frames. New Kingdom, Dynasty XVIII, c. 1348–1335 B.C.; limestone; Boston, Museum of Fine Arts

Temple relief from Amarna
One of the most popular themes in temple reliefs in Amarna is the natural world. The world of animals and plants is an immediate expression of the presence of the sun god on earth. As well as being a purely descriptive listing of the variety of creation, the Amarna reliefs also have great movement, which gives them a certain impressionistic charm.
New Kingdom, Dynasty XVIII, c. 1348–1335 B.C.; limestone; New York, The Metropolitan Museum of Art

Standing figure of King Akhenaten
As in the relief scenes of nature, portraits of the ruler and his family are also very oriented to this world, rather than the next. Akhenaten was not shown in an idealised form, but in an exaggerated form of his real image, thus creating a new artistic standard.
From Amarna; New Kingdom, Dynasty XVIII, c. 1345 B.C.; limestone; Cairo, Egyptian Museum

CASTLES OF ETERNITY

Temples of the Dead and Tomb Architecture of the New Kingdom

Thebes

"For the Aten, my Father" was the dedication on the temples built by Akhenaten in Amarna. According to the wall reliefs, the king, accompanied by the royal family, played the role of the high priest in these temples, and was the only person in direct contact with the Aten. It is not known whether Akhenaten also planned a temple complex for the pursuit of a funerary cult, in addition to the royal tomb. A funerary cult in the traditional sense would seem to have little meaning in a theology that saw the fulfilment of life under the rays of the Aten, in other words in the span between birth and death.

At the end of the Amarna period the royal court moved to Memphis and from then on Egypt's capital was to remain in the north. However, Thebes won back its significance as a spiritual centre in the country and its regained tradition was so strong that Akhenaten's successors and all the rulers of the now commencing Ramesside period, of Dynasties XIX and XX (1307–1070 B.C.) had themselves buried in Thebes, in the Valley of the Kings.

Their rock-cut tombs also comprised a mortuary temple which was located at a considerable distance from the actual tomb, on the edge of the cultivated land. It had already been the practice amongst kings of Dynasty XVIII to have mortuary temples built with their tombs, and these had been arrayed in chronological order from north to south on the western edge of the valley opposite Thebes; the first row contains the temples of Amenhotep I to Horemheb, the second parallel row contains those of Sethos I to the rulers of Dynasty XX. The Ancient Egyptian description of these mortuary temples as "Castles of Eternity" refers to their religious function. They were temples in which the dead king would become one with the King of the gods, with Amun-Re. Here he overcame his mortality and attained a new divinity in colossal statues.

The plan of the temples follows the pattern of an axial sequence of pylons, courts, columned hall, hall with sacrificial altars, audience hall and inner sanctuary. The sanctuary is dedicated to Amun-Re, who, in the form of a temple statue, left the Temple of Karnak once every year and visited his House of Eternity on the other bank of the Nile. In the secondary axis is the sanctuary for the dead king, sometimes also for the royal ancestors. In order to be able to convert the millions of years of rule granted to the king by Amun-Re into a never-ending reign in the other world, the king also had a part of the mortuary temple constructed as a cult palace, a copy of his royal palace. The fusion of king and god ensured that the cult would continue, and to help in its perpetuation a whole range of buildings was built around the temple – storehouses, stables, offices and accommodation for the temple priests.

Only very little remains of almost all the Houses of Eternity of Dynasty XVIII. Of the largest of these, the almost 700-m long complex at the mortuary temple of Amenhotep III (1390–1353 B.C.), all that is left are two colossal statues that once flanked the entrance: the Colossi of Memnon. Just a century and a half after its construction the temple was being used as a quarry, probably because of an earthquake, and material from it was used to build structures and statues for the nearby mortuary temple of King Merenptah (1224–1214 B.C.).

Only one of the royal mortuary temples of Dynasty XVIII in Thebes is still largely intact today, and that is the Temple of Queen Hatshepsut (1473–1458 B.C.) in Deir el-Bahari. It is unusual not only for its remarkable condition, but also for its architectural form, and as such it is therefore not very illuminating as regards the architecture of the destroyed buildings of its predecessors and successors.

The unusual form of Queen Hatshepsut's temple can be explained by the choice of location, in the valley basin of Deir el-Bahari, surrounded by steep cliffs. It was here, in about 2050 B.C., that Mentuhotep II, the founder of the Middle Kingdom, laid out his sloping, terrace-shaped mortuary temple; this terrace structure determined the form of the Hatshepsut temple. The pillared galleries at either side of the central ramp form the rear walls of both courts, and as such correspond to the pillar positions on two successive levels of the Temple of Mentuhotep. Also, the way in which the sanctuary and the side chapels of the Temple of Hatshepsut extend into the rock, forming a hemispeos, a half rock-cut sanctuary, is seen, too, in Mentuhotep's tomb, which is cut deep into the cliff behind the temple.

From a functional and typological point of view the individual parts of the Temple of Hatshepsut correspond to the classical form of Theban mortuary temples: pylon, courts, hypostyle hall (here as a columned court), sun court, chapel for the royal cult, cult palace and sanctuary. As unusual as the architecture are the

General plan of Thebes
While the east bank, with the ancient town of Thebes, is typified by the temples to the gods at the modern locations of Karnak and Luxor, the west bank is the kingdom of the dead. In a long line along the edge of the valley are the royal mortuary temples, and to the west of them the necropolises of the officials, and, in the mountains, the tombs of the kings and queens.

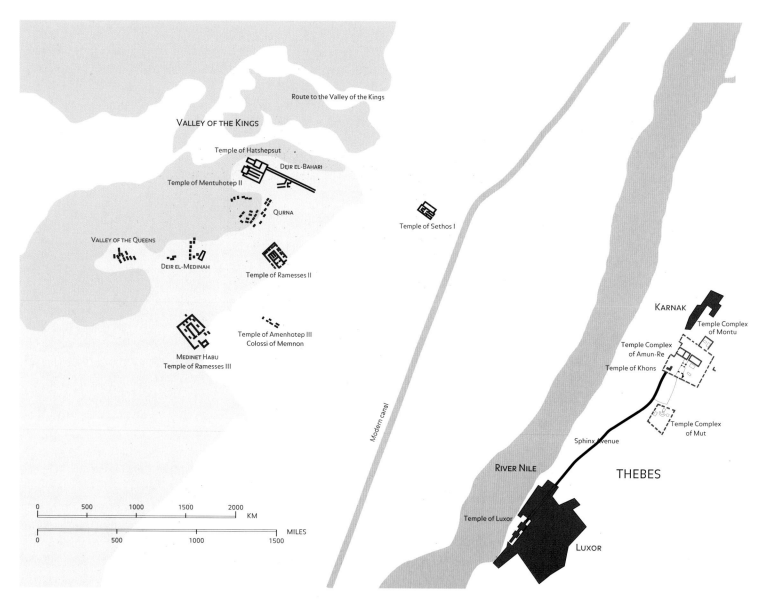

VALLEY OF THE KINGS

Route to the Valley of the Kings

Temple of Hatshepsut

DEIR EL-BAHARI

Temple of Mentuhotep II

QURNA

VALLEY OF THE QUEENS

DEIR EL-MEDINAH

Temple of Ramesses II

Temple of Sethos I

Temple of Amenhotep III
Colossi of Memnon

MEDINET HABU
Temple of Ramesses III

Modern canal

KARNAK

Temple Complex of Montu

Temple Complex of Amun-Re

Temple of Khons

Temple Complex of Mut

Sphinx Avenue

RIVER NILE

THEBES

Temple of Luxor

LUXOR

| 0 | 500 | 1000 | 1500 | 2000 |
KM

| 0 | 500 | 1000 | 1500 |
MILES

Colossi of Memnon

The only remaining part of the largest of the Theban mortuary temples, that of Amenhotep III, are the colossal statues that once flanked the entrance. The northernmost of the monolithic statues was restored under Roman rule and some new blocks were added. New Kingdom, Dynasty XVIII, c. 1360 B.C.; quartzite

themes taken up in the temple reliefs. For the first time in Egyptian art, text and a pictorial cycle tell of the divine birth of the king and also give a detailed pictorial account of an expedition to Punt, the land of incense on the coast of the Red Sea.

Today the terrace temple of Deir el-Bahari can only convey a faint impression of the original intentions of its architect, Senenmut. All the statue ornaments are missing – the statues of Osiris in front of the pillars of the upper colonnade, the sphinx avenues in the court and the standing, sitting and kneeling figures of the queen; all were destroyed in a posthumous condemnation of the queen. The architecture of the temple has been considerably altered as a result of misguided reconstruction in the early part of the twentieth century A.D. It will take many years before current work by a Polish team can at least in part re-create its original appearance.

A representative example of the temples in Dynasty XIX is the mortuary temple of Ramesses II, the Ramesseum, not least because of its impressive colossal statue remains and its well preserved ancillary buildings.

The Houses of Eternity are not restricted to Thebes and not all are close to the royal tombs to which they belong. The fusion of king and god can also take place in

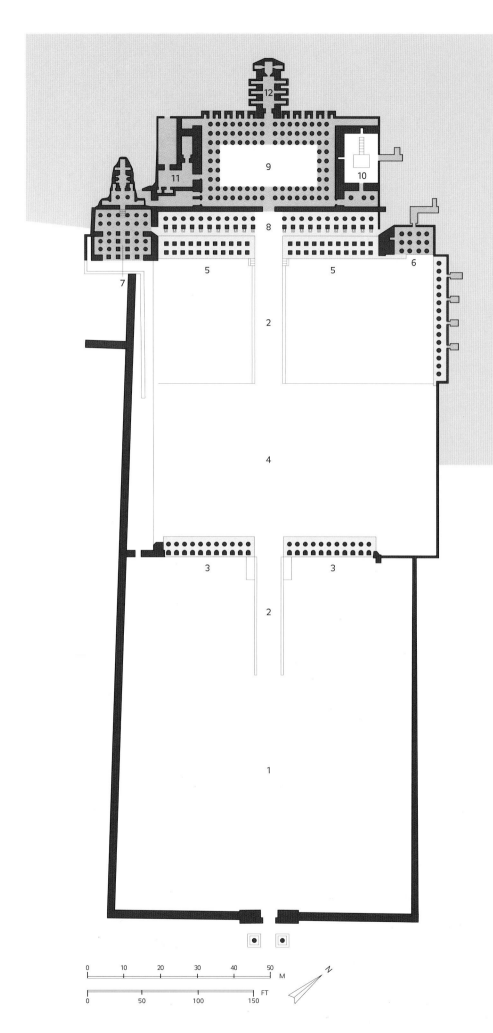

Statue of Queen Hatshepsut
The central axis of the terrace temple of Hatshepsut was an avenue lined with trees and a variety of statues of the queen, either standing, seated or kneeling, or depicted as a sphinx. These figures show her in the full regalia of a pharaoh.
New Kingdom, Dynasty XVIII, c. 1470 B.C.; granite; New York, The Metropolitan Museum of Art

Mortuary temple of Hatshepsut

The original appearance of this terraced temple has been impaired by restoration work carried out in the early twentieth century. A true picture will only emerge after completion of the work of a Polish archaeological team. The colossal column figures of Hatshepsut are to be replaced in front of the columns on the upper terrace, which will break up the rigid line of the architecture.
New Kingdom, Dynasty XVIII, c. 1470 B.C.

Mortuary temple of Queen Hatshepsut, shrine of Anubis

In the northwest corner of the first terrace is a small shrine to Anubis. Its architectural form corresponds to Anubis' character as a god of the underworld. Behind a forecourt with sixteen-sided pillars is an underground sanctuary cut deep into the mountainside.
New Kingdom, Dynasty XVIII, c. 1470 B.C.

Page 132 left

Plan of the mortuary temple of Queen Hatshepsut

The temple complex rises up two terraces from the court to the inner sanctuary, which is hewn out of the rock face. A ramp links the two terraces. Four small shrines are associated with the main temple. 1. Outer court, 2. Ramps, 3. Lower colonnades, 4. Lower terrace, 5. Upper colonnades, 6. Chapel of Anubis, 7. Chapel of Hathor, 8. Pillar of Osiris, 9. Ceremonial court, 10. Sun temple, 11. Chapel of Hatshepsut, 12. Inner sanctuary

Page 132 below right

Kneeling figure of Senmut

Senmut, the Overseer of Works for Queen Hatshepsut, is depicted in reliefs and named in inscriptions as the creator of the Hatshepsut Temple. There are also many statues of him. No fewer than twenty-five statues have survived, including a number showing him as a kneeling figure with the cult symbol of the goddess Hathor. From Armant; New Kingdom, Dynasty XVIII, c. 1470 B.C.; granite; Munich, Staatliche Sammlung Ägyptischer Kunst

Mortuary temple of Queen Hatshepsut, shrine of Hathor
The shape of the pillars of the shrine of Hathor is based on the sistrum, the cult symbol of the goddess Hathor. On the front and back of the capitals is the face of the goddess, with the ears of a cow. On top of the head are stylised cow's horns and between them the façade of a shrine with two uraeuses.
New Kingdom, Dynasty XVIII, c. 1470 B.C.

Relief from the mortuary temple of Queen Hatshepsut
The relief decoration of the Temple of Hatshepsut differs from the standard pictorial programme in that, instead of the usual sacrificial scenes, it contains long picture sequences with unusual themes. An expedition to Punt, the land of incense, the myth of the divine birth of the queen and the transportation of an obelisk are all depicted, as well as several ceremonial processions with parading soldiers.
New Kingdom, Dynasty XVIII, c. 1470 B.C.

Reconstruction of the mortuary temple of Ramesses II (Ramesseum)

While the tombs of the kings of the New Kingdom are situated in remote places in the midst of the Theban mountains, the mortuary temples belonging to them were built at the point where the Nile valley meets the desert. These temples were in fact entire complexes, complete with working quarters, and they functioned as independent administrative units.

Second court of the mortuary temple of Ramesses II (Ramesseum)

On the north and south side of the second court of the Ramesseum stand papyrus columns with closed capitals; on the east and west wall, however, are statue pillars of the king. Their mummy-like form comes from the pillar figures of the king in ceremonial dress, such as are first seen in large scale in the ceremonial court of King Djoser in Saqqara.
New Kingdom, Dynasty XIX, c. 1250 B.C.

Relief wall in the Ramesseum
While the wall reliefs inside the temple depict only religious themes, the outer walls and the walls of the court show scenes of historic events. Ramesses II had the historic Battle of Kadesh depicted on the walls of several temples. The large-scale pictorial account of this battle, in which, in the eighth year of his reign, Ramesses vanquished the king of the Hittites, do not follow the customary format and extend instead over the whole wall.
New Kingdom, Dynasty XIX, c. 1250 B.C.

Page 137
Wall relief in the Hypostyle Hall of the Ramesseum
On the wall at the left side of the southern end of the Hypostyle Hall in the Ramesseum is a large-format relief picture of Ramesses II (on the left) shown approaching the divine couple Amun and Mut; the god-king hands Ramesses II the curved sword and the palm branch as insignia of rule.
New Kingdom, Dynasty XIX, c. 1250 B.C.

Storerooms in the Ramesseum
All around the temple are the workshops, stables, storehouses and apartments of the temple officials. Although only built of unfired mud bricks, their barrel vaults are well preserved and give an authentic impression of how this area used to look.
New Kingdom, Dynasty XIX, c. 1250 B.C.

other important cult places, with the local divinity there. In this context, Osiris, the god of the underworld and of resurrection, was of particular interest to the kings of Dynasty XIX. In addition to their Theban mortuary temples, Ramesses I, Sethos I and Ramesses II also had Houses of Eternity built in Abydos. The reliefs in the Temple of Ramesses II at Abydos are very well preserved and give us insight into the pictorial programme. The external walls have historical scenes showing the Battle of Kadesh in which Ramesses II conquered the king of the Hittites. Inside the temple religious themes dominate. On the walls of the courts are pictures of processions of priests and sacrificial animals. At the base of the walls in the hypostyle hall are reliefs depicting personifications of the districts of Upper and Lower Egypt, thus forming the geopolitical basis for the encounter of god and king, which is seen taking place in the relief pictures above. Here, as in the nearby Temple of Sethos I, the iconography contains many details of the posthumous deification of the pharaoh. In both temples there are also lists of kings dating back to the beginning of Egyptian history in about 3000 B.C.

The biggest House of Eternity was built by Ramesses III; his Theban mortuary temple complex in Medinet Habu is the size of a small town on a site measuring 205 x 315 m. The choice of location in the south of Western Thebes was determined by an ancient shrine there to a snake-like god of creation; this shrine stands in the outer court of the temple of Medinet Habu as a venerable monument to an illustrious past. The approach to the temple complex is via a high gateway in the form of a fortress tower. Another element of secular architecture is the temple palace on the south side of the temple; although it was only designed as a cult building, it is in fact a reproduction of the real palace, even down to details like the sanitary facilities.

The actual mortuary temple, closely related to the Ramesseum in design and wall reliefs, is a classic monumental example of a temple to the gods, with its sequence of two pylons, two courts, a hypostyle hall and the inner sanctuary for Amun, as well as colourful and very well preserved wall reliefs. The pictorial programme in the secondary axes shows the temple's role as a mortuary temple for Ramesses III. In the vignettes of the Book of the Dead Ramesses is shown as a dead person, who, after submitting to the Judgement of the Dead, as all mortals must, is then taken up into the Elysian fields, into the paradise of the gods. The historical reliefs on the seemingly endless outer walls show Ramesses III's battle against the Sea Peoples, a pictorial composition of great narrative dynamism and precise historical detail.

Relief in the Temple of Ramesses II in Abydos
The reliefs in the lowermost friezes in temples often depict personifications of the districts and towns of Egypt. The name of the place in question is written on the headdress of each figure, and in their arms they carry offerings from the land; in this way they symbolise the order of nature as one of the fundamentals of life. New Kingdom, Dynasty XIX, c. 1250 B.C.

Columned hall of the Ramesseum
The architectural scheme of the columned hall in Karnak is found again in the Ramesseum. On both sides of the three raised central aisles, with their columns topped with open papyrus capitals, are the lower side aisles, with closed papyrus capitals. This structural principle is well illustrated here as the outer wall on the south side of the hall has been destroyed. New Kingdom, Dynasty XIX, c. 1250 B.C.

Plan of the Ramesseum
At the southern end of the first court, leading off the axial temple sequence of pylon, two courts, columned hall and sanctuary with anterooms, is the cult palace. The temple on the north wall is probably a birth house. It is not known why this plan deviates from a right angle.

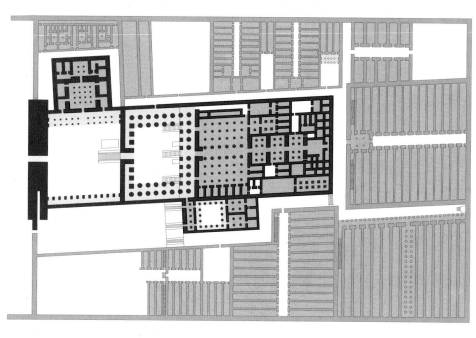

0   10   20   30   40   50
                                M

0   50   100   150   FT

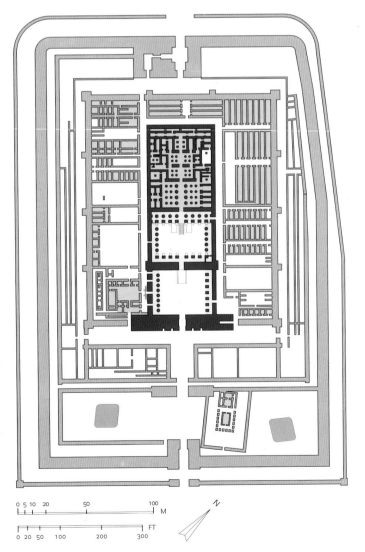

Mortuary temple of Ramesses III
At the southern end of the long
row of Theban mortuary temples
is Medinet Habu, the mortuary
temple of Ramesses III. The choice
of location is influenced by an
older temple (left), built to vener-
ate a snake-like god of earlier
times.
New Kingdom, Dynasty XX,
c. 1150 B.C.

**Plan of the temple of Medinet
Habu**
In plan the mortuary temple of
Ramesses III is only slightly different to the Ramesseum, which also
provided inspiration for the
themes in the temple reliefs.

Page 141
**Colonnade in the second court
of Medinet Habu**
The paintings on the walls,
columns and ceilings in Medinet
Habu are remarkably well preserved and they give a good impression of the bright colours used
on Ramesside reliefs.
New Kingdom, Dynasty XX,
c. 1150 B.C.

Door lintel in the temple of Medinet Habu
Spreading above the doorway are the wings of the sun disc, a symbol of the god Horus since the beginning of Egyptian history. The names of Ramesses III are placed immediately next to this and thereby take on the same cosmic symbolism.
New Kingdom, Dynasty XX, c. 1150 B.C.

The High Gate of Medinet Habu
This gateway construction, several stories high, forms the entrance to the temple complex of Medinet Habu. It is an example of a form used in secular building, in fortifications, adopted for use in sacred architecture. As in the case of the cult palace, the king is presented with an image of earthly reality for his life in the afterworld.
New Kingdom, Dynasty XX, c. 1150 B.C.

Cult palace in Medinet Habu
Built against the south wall of the temple of Medinet Habu, between the first and second pylons, is a small palace, which is associated with the window of appearances in the first court. This break in the wall mimics the audience window of the royal palace and, like its model, is decorated with programmatic scenes of the king destroying the enemies of Egypt.
New Kingdom, Dynasty XX, c. 1150 B.C.

Cult palace in Medinet Habu
Not only the columned hall and throne room (with throne platform) are re-created in the cult palace, but also the sanitary installations. The palace was never intended to be inhabited in real life, it was available solely for the use of the dead king. Cult palaces are found in many mortuary temples in Thebes.
New Kingdom, Dynasty XX, c. 1150 B.C.

Relief in the temple of Medinet Habu

The battle scenes on the outer walls and in the courts in Medinet Habu contain many new individual motifs which depict the horrors of war in a very unusual way. After winning a battle the hands (in some pictures also the genitals) of the fallen were hacked off, piled up in front of the king and counted.
New Kingdom, Dynasty XX, c. 1150 B.C.

Relief on the first pylon of Medinet Habu

The Egyptian king as ruler of the world vanquishes not only the country's enemies, but also destroys evil in nature. War and the hunt are two variants of the religious duty of the king in creating order. The bull hunt depicted on the back of the first pylon in Medinet Habu corresponds typologically to the scene on the front of the pylon, depicting enemies being vanquished.
New Kingdom, Dynasty XX, c. 1150 B.C.

Reconstruction of the temple complex of Medinet Habu
The fortress-like wall with the High Gate surrounds the mortuary temple of Ramesses III and also the older temples in the north-eastern corner; cult rituals continued to be practised in this shrine through into the Roman period.

Wall relief in the temple of Medinet Habu
In the southern part of the mortuary temple of Ramesses III a separate sequence of rooms is reserved for the cult of the dead king. In the wall reliefs Ramesses is seen in the context of the Book of the Dead, working in the fields and praying to the Nile god Hapi and to the Benu bird, the "father of the gods".
New Kingdom, Dynasty XX, c. 1150 B.C.

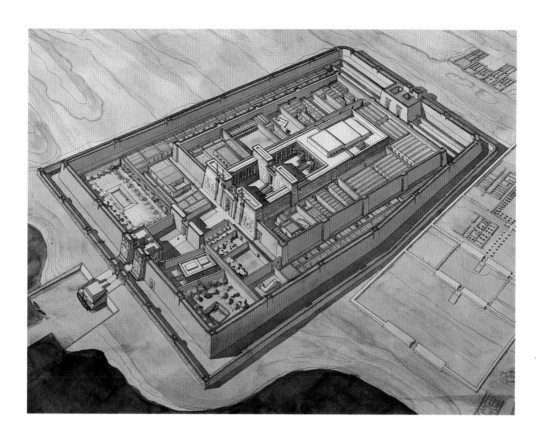

The temples of Abu Simbel in their
new location
Originally the temples of Abu Simbel were situated on the steep
rocky sides of the Nile valley in
Nubia. Today they are 60 m higher
up, above the "Nubian Sea", the
dam which stretches 500 km
southwards from Aswan.
New Kingdom, Dynasty XIX,
c. 1250 B.C.

Page 146
Heads of the colossal statues of
Ramesses II in Abu Simbel
The divine aspects of Egyptian
kingship become the main theme
in the iconography of the Nubian
temples of Ramesses II. The colossal statues on the façade of the
Great Temple of Abu Simbel –
seen here during relocation – are
images of the deified king.
New Kingdom, Dynasty XIX,
c. 1250 B.C.

Rock-Cut Temples

The two functions typical of Egyptian temples from the early days are particularly
evident in the Theban mortuary temples. To the outside the temple is an instrument
for the self-portrayal of royal power. The traditional motif in pylon decoration is the
pharaoh setting out to destroy the enemies of Egypt – a heraldic threatening gesture with no reference to a particular historic incident, but full of political symbolism. Inside the temple the king and the god enter into an indissoluble union; the
god-like persona of the pharaoh guarantees order in the world.

The rock-cut temple, an especially popular structure in Ramesside times, is a particularly good illustration of this double function. Typical of a number of rock-cut
temples in Egypt and Lower Nubia are two shrines erected by Ramesses II in Abu
Simbel, 300 km south of the actual border of the Empire at the First Cataract, in a
part of the Nile valley only thinly populated with Nubians. The colossal seated statues of Ramesses II on the façade of the larger temple and the standing figures of the
king and Queen Nefertari in front of the smaller temple of Abu Simbel are self-por-
trayals of the deified royal couple, who in the form of these gigantic images seek to
secure the borders of the empire. The question as to whether the statues in the
smaller temple in Abu Simbel represent Queen Nefertari in the form of the goddess
Hathor, or whether the goddess here takes on human form as the queen, is imma-
terial. Queen and goddess have become one.

The architecture of the rock-cut temple pushes its way into the rock itself, into
the subterranean part, beyond the borders of the accessible world into the

Page 149

Colossal statues of Ramesses II in Abu Simbel

The four colossal statues of Ramesses II are 22 m high. They are hewn directly out of the rock face on the façade of the Great Temple of Abu Simbel. The combination of king's headdress and double crown of Upper and Lower Egypt is also found in other colossal statues of the king. The flatness of the face is underlined by the wide ceremonial beard and the bulky uraeus.
New Kingdom, Dynasty XIX, c. 1250 B.C.

The Great Temple of Abu Simbel

In the case of a rock-cut temple the "standard" elements of an Egyptian temple are located further back in the projecting rock face. The façade of the Great Temple of Abu Simbel is formed like a pylon tower with sloping walls, roll moulding and cavetto. The colossal statues of Ramesses II hewn out of the rock face are the same in typological terms as free-standing statues, such as the ones in front of the temple of Luxor. The typical relief decoration of the pylon front is moved back inside the temple; the scene showing the king vanquishing enemies is found on the wall of the entrance to the underground court.
New Kingdom, Dynasty XIX, c. 1250 B.C.

Wall relief in the Great Temple of Abu Simbel
Ramesses II is shown praying to three gods. The god in the middle is a representation of himself in divine form, flanked on either side by Amun and Mut. The sun disk and ram's horns are divine attributes not normally associated with royal regalia.
From: I. Rosellini, *Monumenti dell' Egitto e della Nubia,* 1832–1844

Sanctuary of the Great Temple of Abu Simbel
The three gods, Ptah (not illustrated here), Amun and Re-Harakhty, the gods of Memphis, Thebes and Heliopolis, are joined in the inner sanctuary of the Great Temple of Abu Simbel by the deified form of Ramesses II, who has taken his place alongside the gods.
New Kingdom, Dynasty XIX, c. 1250 B.C.

Page 151
Hall of the Great Temple of Abu Simbel
Statue pillars are typical architectural elements in temple courtyards. When found in the large underground entrance hall of the Great Temple of Abu Simbel, they thus define this hall as a court. The ceiling decoration with vultures spreading their wings is a representation of the skies spanning the open court.
New Kingdom, Dynasty XIX, c. 1250 B.C.

Plan and longitudinal section of the Great Temple of Abu Simbel
The storerooms which in the case of a free-standing temple are placed around the temple building, occur in the Great Temple of Abu Simbel as underground chambers. The cult scenes in the wall reliefs of these rooms indicate more of a ritualistic than a practical function.

Small Temple of Abu Simbel
A statue of Queen Nefertari is placed between each of the two colossal stepping-standing figures of Ramesses II. She wears a Hathor crown to indicate her status as a deified queen. The niche structure underlines the function of the rock-cut temple as the boundary between the upper and the lower worlds, between the profane outside and the sacred inside.
New Kingdom, Dynasty XIX, c. 1250 B.C.

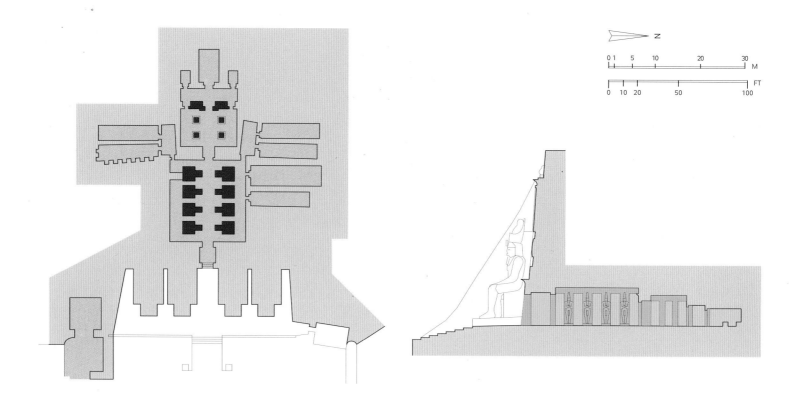

Pillared hall in the Small Temple of Abu Simbel
Hathor pillars are found in the Small Temple in Abu Simbel. Here, as with the pillar figures of the deified Ramesses, the Hathor emblem of the sistrum becomes the image of the deified queen, whose coronation as a goddess is depicted in the sanctuary.
New Kingdom, Dynasty XIX, c. 1250 B.C.

unknown, the underworld, and as such is the architectural expression of the inter-linking of the worlds above and below ground, of the secular and the sacred, of king and god. The mystery of caves, which in many cultures has been the impetus for cre-ating cave shrines, was also the moving force in Ancient Egypt behind the creation of special sanctuaries in underground places to ease the king's passage into the world of the gods. In no other place is Ramesses II depicted in statues and reliefs so often and so clearly with the insignia of divinity, as in the rock-cut temples of Nubia.

The essential function of a temple as a place where the king as the representative of humanity comes into direct contact with the gods, is here the sole task of archi-tecture. The fact that in the thinly populated area of Nubia there were very few people to receive this message from the divine pharaoh, was of little significance in terms of the building's ability to perform its function. The statement made by its architectural form, its wall reliefs and statues is inherent within the building itself; it creates its own reality and needs no observer to ensure its effectiveness or func-tion.

Quarry and Drawing-Board – Construction Planning and Logistics

Stone quarry at Gabal el-Silsila
From the days of the New Kingdom onwards sandstone for building all the Upper Egyptian temples came from the quarries at Gabal el-Silsila to the south of Edfu. Still today we can see the evidence of ancient quarrying on the rock face, which in places reaches 20 m in height.

In a quarry in Wadi Hammamat
In the eastern desert between the Nile valley and the Red Sea are greywacke quarries; this rock was a favourite material for statues and sarcophagi. Unfinished blocks lay in the places where they were worked.

For many decades research in Egyptology has devoted little attention to the practical aspects of Ancient Egyptian architecture. The effect on the visitor of the sheer physical presence of the pyramids and temples is so hypnotic that all questions concerning quarrying and transport of material, technology and organisation and planning are pushed into the background. At the most there has been wild speculation about how these gigantic building feats were performed.

A systematic investigation into the quarries of the Nile valley in Egypt is now giving precise details on the origin of the stones used in the time of the pharaohs, and on the quarrying techniques employed. Some of the ancient quarries between Cairo and Aswan have survived unchanged to the present day, because they have been unused since Ancient Egyptian times. Limestone quarries, mostly in the form of underground cave quarries, are found from Gebel Mokattam near Cairo through the whole of Middle Egypt up to the area around Luxor. A particularly valued form of limestone, calcite-alabaster, was quarried, among other places, in open-cast mines in Hat-nub near Amarna. Basalt quarries are found to the north of the Fayum oasis near Kasr el-Sagha. Quartzite was quarried both at Gebel el-Ahmar, the "red mountain" on

the eastern outskirts of modern-day Cairo, and on the west bank of the Nile near Aswan. Anorthosite gneiss, known as "Chephren diorite", comes from a quarry in Nubia, far into the desert to the south-west of Abu Simbel. The composition of the stone in the various buildings and statues enables conclusions to be drawn as to their places of origin, and also enables quarrying dates to be established.

To the south of Edfu in Upper Egypt, for a distance of several kilometres close by the Nile on both banks, are the sandstone quarries of Gabal el-Silsila which were used from about 2000 B.C. to the days of the Roman empire to provide building material for the large temple complexes in Upper Egypt, including, for example, Karnak, the Ramesseum, Medinet Habu, Dendera, Esna, Edfu and Kom Ombo. The cliff faces in this open-cast mine reach 30 m in height, showing where shafts were cut vertically into the rock. Markings left in the rock give information on the tools used (bronze and iron chisels) and on the dimensions of blocks hewn here. The layout of the quarry site shows that loading ramps were constructed in ravines cut deep into the rock from the river's edge up to the mine shafts, and that some quarries, at least in times of flood, had a direct canal link to the Nile. This meant that the sandstone

blocks only had to be manoeuvred a short distance before loading onto river barges. The further transport of these blocks was aided by the fact that the quarries were generally upriver of the building sites, so the heavy barges could just be steered along on the river current.

Unfinished work pieces found still lying in the quarries show that the basic outline of statues and architectural components were hewn at the quarry site itself, in order to save weight in transport. It seems therefore that work was done to order for specific commissions, and that there was no "stockpile" of hewn blocks.

Quarrying was not so straightforward everywhere as it was in Gabal el-Silsila. Rarer hard rocks, such as the greenish greywacke popular for use in statues or sarcophagi, had to be quarried in the eastern desert, in a region which was still in active use in later times; the Roman emperors quarried red porphyry here and transported it in great quantities as far as Rome and Byzantium. The expedition leaders were faced with an enormous challenge in terms of transporting the material 100 km to the Nile valley, feeding and accommodating hundreds of workers and all the other administrative problems of organising a large-scale operation in inhospitable and difficult terrain in the desert

Stone quarries in the Egyptian Nile valley

Along its whole length from Aswan to Cairo the Nile valley has ancient stone quarries. Sandstone was quarried in the south and limestone to the north of Edfu. Hard stone was extracted in Aswan, in the eastern desert, in the Fayum and at the southern tip of the Delta.

Papyrus with site plan of a quarry

This ancient map drawn on papyrus was used in finding the way in the rough terrain of the eastern desert. It is thought to show a part of the Wadi Hammamat. New Kingdom, Dynasties XIX/XX, 1300–1100 B.C. Turin, Museo Egizio

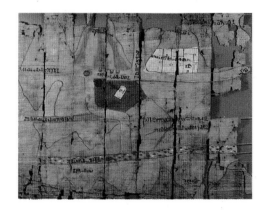

mountains between the Nile valley and the Red Sea. It was not without a certain pride that they told in long inscriptions of their achievements, complete with interesting information about numbers employed, equipment used and the type and quantity of blocks hewn, some of which reached a weight of 50 tons.

The largest stone monuments came from the area around the First Cataract near Aswan; since the days of the Old Kingdom monolithic obelisks were made from rose granite typical of the Aswan region. The largest known obelisk never left the quarry, and today still lies unfinished in its ancient workshop. At about 1200 tons in weight, it seems to have overtaxed the technical capabilities of the New Kingdom.

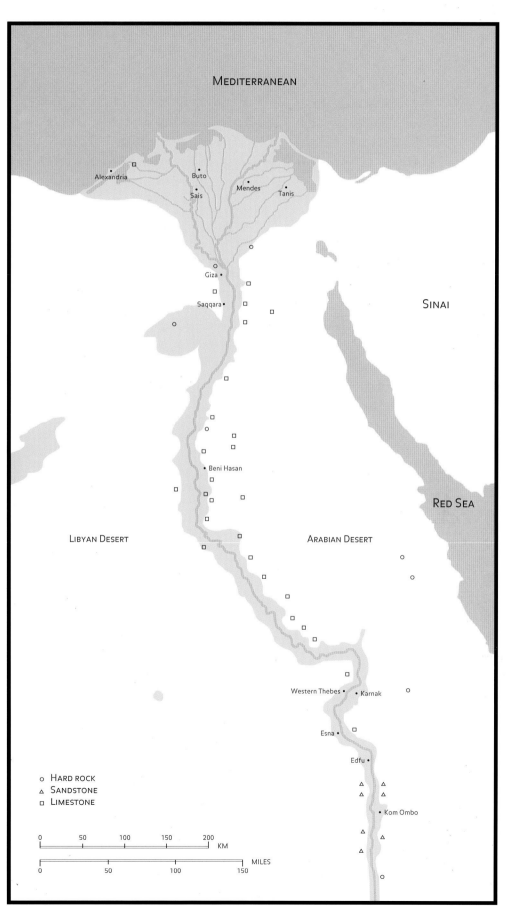

MEDITERRANEAN

Alexandria
Buto
Sais
Mendes
Tanis

SINAI

Giza

Saqqara

Beni Hasan

LIBYAN DESERT

ARABIAN DESERT

RED SEA

Western Thebes • Karnak

Esna

Edfu

Kom Ombo

○ HARD ROCK
△ SANDSTONE
□ LIMESTONE

0   50   100   150   200   KM

0   50   100   150   MILES

The overland transport of heavy loads is depicted in tomb reliefs. The vehicle used for this form of transport was a flat, wooden sled with wide runners, and it was pulled by workers or by cattle used as draught animals. A key part of the process was the construction of a path along which the load could be dragged; a layer of mud from the Nile spread along the route meant that even the heaviest loads could be moved more easily. For raising heavy loads, ramps were built and the load dragged up on runners. The remains of such ramps can still be seen at the First Pylon in Karnak, the pyramid of Medum and in many other structures.

We can have no illusions about working conditions at the larger building sites, during transport of the blocks and in the quarries. Despite the claims of the expedition leaders that all the workers returned unharmed from the quarries, we can assume that the accident and death rates were high. Ancient Egyptian representations often depict the workers as members of lower social groups, or as non-Egyptians, many of whom would have been prisoners of war.

Only little is known about construction planning in Ancient Egypt. The "anonymous" architecture of ordinary houses, villages and towns would simply have sprung up spontaneously and organically from the specifics of the local situation, but basic temple forms changed little over the course of millennia, indicating that certain guidelines must have existed. For the individual building components such as pillars, doors and naoi, there are many models and drawings still in existence, either on papyrus or on ostraca, but

general plans or models of whole buildings are rare. Precise drawings with written descriptions of two royal tombs have survived, those of Ramesses IV and Ramesses IX, in the Valley of the Kings; however, these plans are more like records of finished tombs than plans for use during construction. The same is true of the few temple models which were probably intended as votive offerings and not as actual construction aids. Real construction sketches giving dimensions of vault structures and angles of inclination of pyramids are still the exception.

In addition to drawings of buildings there are also descriptions which allow us to reconstruct a detailed picture of the furniture and fittings in the temples. Although temples such as those at Medinet Habu and Abydos still give a very vivid impression as a result of their coloured wall reliefs, they nevertheless lack key elements necessary for the overall effect of an Ancient Egyptian shrine. The *Harris I Papyrus* from Dynasty XX contains descriptions of the temple buildings of Ramesses III and its associated donations. Again and again, in the descriptions of temples in Thebes and Memphis, Heliopolis and many other towns in Egypt, we read of "gates of electrum and hammered copper", of "windows of appearances made of fine gold", of "sacrificial altars of repoussé silver, mounted in gold" and of "gods' barques of 130 cubits in length made of cedar wood, clad to the water line with gold and with a shrine in the centre, made entirely of gold and inlaid with all kinds of precious stones, and with ram's heads of gold from bow to stern". The descriptions contained in these texts of temple

Sketch of a stonemason
Ostraca were not only used by artists for recording their designs, but also as sketchpads, as here. This quick sketch shows a bald-headed, unshaven stonemason working on what is clearly a laborious task.
New Kingdom, Dynasties XIX/XX, c. 1300–1100 B.C.; Cambridge, Fitzwilliam Museum

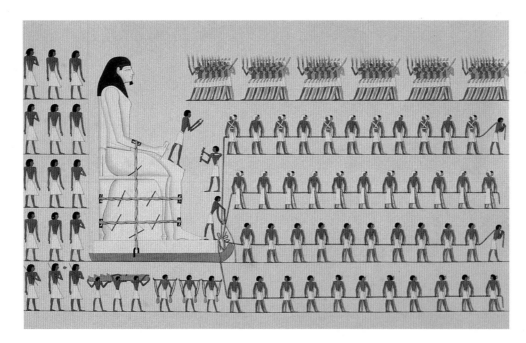

Tomb painting in Deir el-Bersha
In the tomb of Djehuty-hetep in Deir el-Bersha in Central Egypt there is a scene representing the transport of a colossal statue. The heaviest workpieces were transported on wooden sleds with wide runners over a path reinforced with boards and spread with mud. Middle Kingdom, Dynasties XI/XII, c. 1900 B.C.; from: H. v. Minutoli, *Reise zur Oase des Jupiter Ammon,* 1824

Page 156 above
Design for a building

A number of architectural sketches drawn on ostraca, clay or limestone fragments have been found. This hasty sketch on a potsherd is an elevation of a kiosk. New Kingdom, Dynasties XIX/XX, c. 1300–1100 B.C.; Berlin, Ägyptisches Museum

Architectural model of a temple

Architectural projects were also presented in three-dimensional models. Here a quartzite block was used to mark out the locations of the pylon, obelisks, flagpoles, statues and sphinxes for a temple in Heliopolis. The various architectural elements have been reconstructed on the original base. New Kingdom, Dynasty XIX, c. 1290 B.C.; quartzite; New York, The Brooklyn Museum

Inscription in Wadi Hammamat

Here an expedition leader has immortalised himself in an inscription in which he lists his forebears, all of whom were builders. He compares the oldest of them to Imhotep, the builder of the Step Pyramid of Saqqara. Late Period, c. 580 B.C.

walls clad with precious metals are confirmed by the many examples of dowel-holes to be found around reliefs or inscriptions; these were the fixing points for panels of gold and silver sheet. Brightly coloured faience and glass insets heightened the general impression of colourfulness.

The planning and construction of these extremely valuable temples was one of the most responsible and highly respected of state offices. The craft skills and organisational knowledge required for completion of such tasks was passed on by word of mouth within the various professional groups, made up of groups of families. There are many examples of the family trees of master builders, some of which extend over several hundred years back into the earliest period.

The high regard in which the capabilities of the Chief of Works were held and how closely this knowledge and ability was linked to individual leading personalities is shown by the fact that some of them were revered over the course of centuries or even millennia. One such was Imhotep (c. 2650 B.C.) who built the oldest stone pyramid in Egypt, the Step Pyramid of Saqqara, and another was Amenhotep, son of Hapu (c. 1360 B.C.), Chief of Works under Amenhotep III; both men were venerated as shining examples of Ancient Egyptian wisdom until as late as the Ptolemaic and Roman periods. Their achievements in architecture were representative of their role in the culture of Egypt; architecture is the immediate expression of national identity and pride. The position of the architect as a central figure in cultural life can be seen in the biographies of various personalities in Ancient Egyptian history. Senenmut, the Overseer of Works for Queen Hatshepsut (c. 1470 B.C.), built a lasting memorial to himself in the form of the terraced temple of Deir el-Bahari, which he actually built for Hatshepsut and in which he left many examples of his signature in pictures and in text. Thus, from the Ancient Egyptian point of view, the history of Egyptian architecture was for all intents and purposes the history of Egyptian culture itself.

Paths into the Next World

One of the main and most exceptional architectural achievements of the Ancient Egyptians was barely noticed at the time of construction: the royal tombs of the New Kingdom. With the exception of Akhenaten all the rulers of Dynasties XVIII, XIX and XX for a period of about 500 years (1550–1070 B.C.) were buried in underground rock-cut tombs in the Valley of the Kings in Thebes. After burial the entrance to the tomb was covered by a pile of debris which hid all indication of the burial site, and formed a contrast to the royal tomb complexes of the Old and Middle Kingdoms with their towering pyramids, visible from afar, which could hardly have been greater.

The hidden location of the tombs in a rocky desert valley that was difficult to reach and the concealment of the tomb entrances are often explained in terms of security considerations, but reports of tomb robbers in the New Kingdom show that these royal resting places were violated very soon after burial. The change in architectural form has deeper roots; it reflects the changed perspectives of life after death. In place of the pyramid as a symbolic staircase and memorial to the sun, helping the king rise to the gods in the heavens, there were now underground rock-cut tombs representing the underworld spaces traversed by the sun-god during his night-time journey from setting in the evening to rising again each morning in the east. The deceased king, now transformed into Osiris, descends into the night barque of the sun-god Re and, now one with him, travels through the twelve hours of darkness. "Osiris is this that is in Re. Re is this that is in Osiris" – this is how a tomb inscription expressed the underworld union of king and god. The tomb architecture translates these ideas into physical space. Thus the deep vertical shaft located at

Sarcophagus chamber in the tomb of Tuthmosis III in the Valley of the Kings

Deep below the earth in the royal tombs of the New Kingdom in the Valley of the Kings a fictitious afterworld takes on architectural form. Here in the oval room containing the sarcophagus of Tuthmosis III three picture friezes present and describe the twelve hours of the night as a detailed topography of the world beyond. New Kingdom, Dynasty XVIII, c. 1450 B.C.

the end of a steeply sloping entrance corridor to the tomb is not designed as an obstacle for tomb robbers, but represents the "cave of Sokaris", in other words an underworld space through which the deceased must pass. The sarcophagus chamber (oval-shaped until the middle of Dynasty XVIII) is an image of the space for the twelfth hour of the night. The sequence of entrance corridors and columned halls is repeated inside the tombs; the front part of the tomb is dedicated to the dead king as Osiris, the following section to the ruler, now united with the sun-god Re.

The decoding of this symbolism of tomb spaces is made possible through the pictures or inscriptions that cover all the walls and often also the ceilings. Reliefs and paintings depict in at first incomprehensible, bizarre pictures the underworld as a place which can be walked through – it has paths, canals and islands. Each hour of the night has its gateways guarded by fire-spitting snakes and it is populated by demons which the sun-god overcomes, helped by good spirits. At the end of this dangerous journey he, and with him the dead king, emerges successfully as a young

A picture of the underworld in the tomb of Tuthmosis III in the Valley of the Kings
The path of the sun from evening to morning is the cosmic precedent for the king's passage from death to resurrection. The representation of the route leading sharply downwards into the depths of the night is reflected also in the corridors of the tomb driven deep into the rock.
New Kingdom, Dynasty XVIII, c. 1450 B.C.

Ceiling picture in the tomb of Ramesses VI in the Valley of the Kings
The goddess of the heavens, Nut, forms the night sky with her body, along which the barque of the sun travels. The sun, swallowed by Nut in the evening, is born again each morning from her womb. The arched ceiling of the sarcophagus chamber extends the image to cosmic space.
New Kingdom, Dynasty XX, c. 1145 B.C.

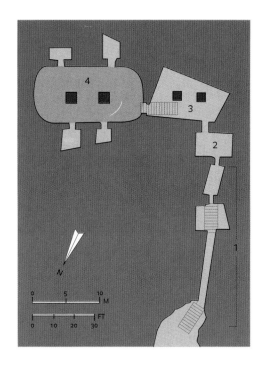

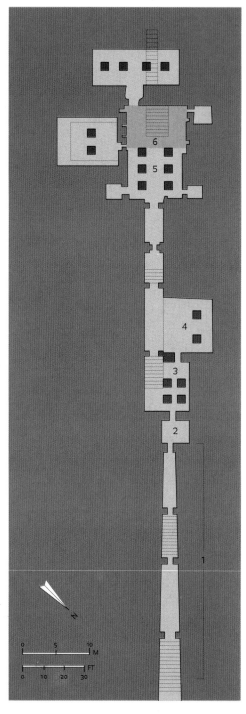

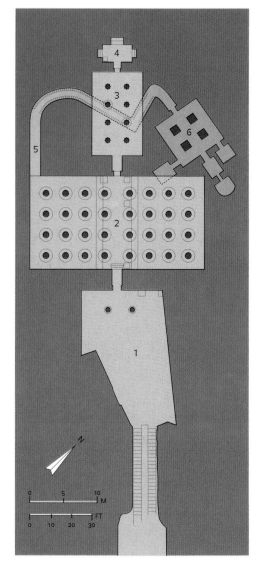

Plans of Theban tombs

Left: Tomb of Tuthmosis III in the Valley of the Kings. The angled axis is typical of royal tombs in the pre-Amarna period. 1. Entrance corridors, 2. Shaft space, 3. Columned hall, 4. Tomb chamber
Centre: Tomb of Sethos I in the Valley of the Kings. After the Amarna period tombs were aligned along a straight axis, with the idea that the sun's rays could reach into the darkness. Half-way between the entrance and the sarcophagus chamber the axis shifts slightly to the side. From here the front section sequence of rooms is repeated. 1. Entrance corridors, 2. Shaft space, 3. Upper columned hall, 4. Upper tomb chamber, 5. Lower columned hall, 6. Tomb chamber

Right: Tomb of Ramose in Gurna. Behind the forecourt the wide hall extends to form a columned hall from where a winding corridor leads to the sarcophagus chamber. 1. Court, 2. Wide hall, 3. Deep hall, 4. Statue chamber, 5. Corridor, 6. Tomb chamber

god on a new day. An alternative picture of the afterworld with a star-studded night sky is presented in the ceilings of the sarcophagus chambers from Dynasty XIX onwards. Vaulting over the sky is the female body of the sky-goddess Nut, through which the sun passes to rise again new-born from her womb in the morning. A characteristic of the royal tombs of the New Kingdom is that, except for the entrance corridor, no wall pictures show representations of the king in his tomb. The dead ruler is consumed entirely by the gods, and the tomb is as a result not so much a burial place for the pharaoh as the architectural representation of a mythical space, an imagined and believed world on the other side of death; it is the concretisation of a landscape not accessible to the senses.

Until just a few years ago Egyptologists were baffled by this architecture and by the wall reliefs in the royal tombs of the New Kingdom, but the work of a few researchers, most importantly the Basle Egyptologist, Erik Hornung, in translating the texts and providing an impartial and objective description of the pictures, has

Tomb of Nefertari in the Valley of the Queens

A special place was reserved in Thebes for the members of the king's family. This "Place of Beauty" is now called the Valley of the Queens. The tomb of Nefertari, the wife of Ramesses II, is notable for the similarity of its layout with that of the kings' tombs, and for its excellent painted reliefs on the walls.
New Kingdom, Dynasty XIX, c. 1250 B.C.

Tomb of Nefertari

The pictorial programme in the tomb of Nefertari combines elements from kings' tombs, private tombs and temple reliefs into a new concept focusing on the communion of the dead queen with the gods.
New Kingdom, Dynasty XIX, c. 1250 B.C.

led the way to an understanding and appreciation of this fascinating world of the imagination.

The tomb of Tutankhamun (c. 1323 B.C.) is the only one of these tombs to have survived almost complete to the present day, and from it we can at least obtain a glimpse of the riches which originally accompanied the kings into the next world. The very fact that all the other tombs were emptied by tomb robbers is an indication of the precious nature of the objects they contained.

The funerary cult for the deceased ruler was performed in his "House of Eternity", his mortuary temple, which lay at a distance from the tomb itself, on the edge of the cultivated land. The priests engaged in the cult of the dead thus had no contact with the actual burial location of the king, and the sacrificial offerings were slaughtered on altars which lay several kilometres from the body of the person whom they were to assist in the other world.

Tombs of higher-ranking citizens of Thebes lie in the rocky hills between the Valley of the Kings and the royal mortuary temples. In contrast to the royal tombs which were unrecognisable from the outside, these tombs have architectural façades with mock doors, stelae and pillars at the back of the courtyards cut into the rocky slope. Above the entrance of some of the tombs is a small, steep-sided pyramid with an east-facing statue niche containing a kneeling figure of the tomb's occupant holding a stela with a hieroglyphic hymn to the rising sun. The reference to the solar aspect of the royal pyramids of the Old and Middle Kingdoms is clear.

Inside the tomb the first room, on a transverse axis, has reliefs and wall paintings with a strongly biographical theme. They tell of the professional career of the tomb's occupant and as such are an inexhaustible pictorial encyclopaedia of the civilisation of the New Kingdom. At right angles to this room, on the same level, is a narrower room cut deeper into the cliff and often leading to a statue niche. The pictures in the front part of this room deal with the burial and the "Beautiful Festival in

Forecourt of a private tomb in Western Thebes
The Theban tombs of the members of the upper classes are found in the rocky cliffs of the steep, western mountains. In front of the underground rock-cut tomb is a forecourt cut out of the mountainside like a terrace. Often stelae were chiselled out of the projecting rock face at the back of the court.

the Desert Valley", a grand annual festival of the dead, by means of which, through much feasting, drinking, music and dance, the division between the living and the dead is removed. The walls in the back part of this room have representations of the deceased's encounter with the gods of the underworld. This part of the tomb is at ground level and was used for carrying out the cult of the dead.

In distinct contrast to these rooms and spatially separate was the sarcophagus chamber which was to be found deep under the earth. The shaft that led down to it was filled after the body was buried, thus making the chamber inaccessible. The walls of the chamber are decorated with pictures of the deceased and his family in communion with the gods. The body itself was contained inside a series of painted wooden coffins, around which was placed the burial objects, furniture and ceramics, jewellery, clothing and fruits of the soil.

In some tombs this underground part is designed to be accessible by means of a gently sloping ramp leading down to the sarcophagus chamber from the tranverse entrance room. The formal analogy to the royal tomb is clear and we can assume that here, too, the idea of an accessible underworld was the determining factor in the architectural design.

More than 400 tombs with reliefs and paintings have so far been uncovered in the Theban necropolis; each year new ones come to light. Yet, despite the shared basic architectural structure and wall-painting themes in these tombs, each one is a distinctive work of art. The artists and craftsmen who created the tombs in the Valley of the Kings lived and were buried in the Deir el-Medinah part of the Theban necropolis, and we can assume that they themselves were responsible for designing their own tombs. The task of distinguishing the various individual styles has yet to be completed.

The remains of a settlement in Deir el-Medinah
The craftsmen and artists who worked in the Valley of the Kings lived in a settlement cut off from the outside world in a mountain valley not far from their place of work. Here, in the well preserved ruins of this craftsmen's village, many texts have been found telling of everyday life and giving us insight into the organisation of work, the level of wages and the private lives of the workers.

After Thebes, the necropolis of Memphis is the most significant example of non-royal tomb architecture of the New Kingdom. The quite different geographical situation here leads to a new building form that differs quite markedly from the Theban tomb type. In place of the rock-cut tomb with an underground section hewn directly out of the cliff, the necropolis of Memphis, at its location within sight of the Step Pyramid of Djoser and the pyramids of Seneferu in Dahshour, features a tomb in the form of a small temple. An entrance pylon leads through into a pillared court (some have several pylons and courts), and behind the court are the shrines for the statues of the deceased and his family members. Above this rear section is a small, steep-sided pyramid. The burial chamber itself is often just one of several levels of underground burial rooms. So far only a small portion of these New-Kingdom tombs in Memphis, mostly the ones south of the causeway to the Pyramid of Unas, have been excavated. One find in particular – the sensational discovery of the tomb of Wesir Aper-el from the time of Amenhotep III and IV – shows how incomplete our knowledge is of this epoch in the necropolis of Memphis.

The heyday of this New-Kingdom necropolis was in the short period at the end of Dynasty XVIII, when Memphis again became the capital of Egypt. Amarna, the former capital, had been abandoned in around 1333 B.C. following the death of Akhenaten and it was not until the beginning of Dynasty XIX, in about 1300 B.C., that the royal residence was transferred to the new capital, the future Ramesside town, in the north-east Nile Delta. Thus it was the highest-ranking officials, after the king, that were buried in the necropolis in Memphis, close to their seat of office. The tomb of the commander of the Egyptian army, General Horemheb, later to take the pharaoh's throne as the soldier king, is also to be found in Saqqara, as well as that of the finance minister Maja; both men held office during the reign of King Tutankhamun. Their tombs thus stand at the junction of the Amarna and Ramesside periods, and their wall reliefs represent the final examples, one can even say the pinnacle, of the stylistic development of Amarna art, before more traditional forms were introduced at the end of Dynasty XVIII with Ramesside classicism.

The large number of tombs with painting and relief decoration in the two necropolises of Thebes and Memphis would tend to suggest that similar cemeteries could be expected at other important towns in the New Kingdom. The poor condition of the tomb complexes in the towns in the Delta (Heliopolis, Bubastis, the city of Ramesses) may well be due to their damp Delta location, but even the Upper

Tomb relief from the necropolis in Memphis
Only in the cemeteries of Thebes and Memphis are there large numbers of tombs whose walls are decorated with long picture cycles. In Saqqara, the necropolis of Memphis, it is the relief picture which dominates. A detail from the tomb of the court jeweller, Imeneminet, shows the deceased in human form and as spirit birds at a pond in the afterworld. New Kingdom, Dynasty XVIII, c. 1320 B.C.; limestone; Munich, Staatliche Sammlung Ägyptischer Kunst

Wall painting in a Theban tomb
In the rock-cut tombs of Thebes most of the wall paintings were applied directly onto plaster. In a picture in the tomb of Nakhtamon in Deir el-Medinah the sarcophagi of the deceased and his wife are shown in front of the tomb's façade, where a sharply pointed pyramid rises above the door to the tomb. The background is an impression of the rocky cliffs of the Theban mountains. New Kingdom, Dynasties XIX/XX, 1200–1150 B.C.

Necropolis of Deir el-Medinah
Just behind the houses of the craftsmen's village of Deir el-Medinah are the entrances to underground tombs cut into the cliff face. Most of the entrances are marked with small, steep-sided pyramids. The sarcophagus chambers lie deep down in the rock below the ground-level cult chamber.

Egyptian towns or larger settlements in Nubia have only few tombs that are comparable with the Theban ones. In Elkab near Edfu in Upper Egypt there are a number of rock-cut tombs from Dynasty XVIII, each one consisting of only one room decorated with painted flat reliefs, and also in Hierakonpolis, near to Elkab on the west bank, there are simple rock-cut tombs with wall paintings. A faint echo of the tradition of rock-cut tombs can also be seen in Aniba and Dibeira in Nubia.

The concentration in Thebes and Memphis of New-Kingdom private tombs with reliefs and wall paintings is in stark contrast to the widespread occurrence of this type of tomb in the Middle Kingdom and leads us to conclude that such tombs in the New Kingdom were the privilege of the political centres and that the relevant artistic skills were only available in those centres. This geographical concentration also explains the completely different architectural types in Thebes and Memphis and the quite unmistakable and distinctive styles of wall decoration in each.

THE COSMOS IN STONE

From the Delta to Sudan

Page 167
Mummy mask of King Psusennes
The kings of the Third Intermediate Period had their tombs built in the temple enclosure of their residence city of Tanis in the Nile Delta. The above-ground structures have been completely destroyed. Here, in around 1940, the grave goods were found intact in the underground sarcophagus room and side chambers. After the tomb of Tutankhamun this is the most important treasure found so far in Egypt.
Third Intermediate Period, Dynasty XXI, c. 1000 B.C.; gold; Cairo, Egyptian Museum

Pectoral of King Amenemope
This chest ornament from the tomb of Amenemope in Tanis shows the sun-god in the form of a beetle between the goddesses Isis and Nephthys. They are surrounded by the architectural framework of a temple crowned with roll moulding and cavetto. In the centre at the top is the winged disc of the sun, such as is found above temple gateways.
Third Intermediate Period, Dynasty XXI, c. 985 B.C.; gold, lapis lazuli, faience; Cairo, Egyptian Museum

Bubastis and Tanis

In Egyptian archaeology the Nile Delta plays a minor role, although it was and still is the largest usable area for settlement and agriculture in the whole of Egypt. This archaeological vacuum has often been explained by the belief that in Ancient Egyptian times much of the Delta consisted of inhospitable swampland, but recent excavations in the last twenty years have proved this assumption to be false. Even as early as the fourth millennium B.C. the Nile Delta had many settlements, and it has been an important economic centre since the days of the Old Kingdom. Throughout the whole of the 3000 year history of the Nile region, original text sources give a vivid and detailed picture of a densely populated Delta region with many towns and villages.

The comparative lack of finds in the Delta is primarily the result of geomorphological conditions, intensive agricultural use and the dense settlement pattern. The archaeologically interesting layers are now in many places located below the water-table and buried under metres of silt deposited there by the annual flooding of the Nile valley. This for the most part makes excavation a technical and financial impossibility. Many of the ancient settlements and cemeteries that were located on higher ground, rising above the valley floor as low mounds, have been flattened to provide more agriculturally usable land. Towns are continually expanding to cope with a rapidly growing population, and in doing so they are covering over and destroying many historical sites. Today the entire Nile Delta can be described as a region in archaeological crisis.

However, the significance of this region in the history of Ancient Egypt justifies a look at the few remains of the once so important towns here. On the southern edge of the city of Zagazig in the eastern Nile Delta are the remains of Bubastis, the town which was dedicated to the cat-goddess, Bastet. The description of the temple, as given by the Greek historian Herodotus, has been confirmed by archaeological excavations. Toppled pillars, architraves and statues of red granite have been found on the 50 x 180 m site of the Bastet temple, constructed in the time of Ramesses II (1290–1224 B.C.), on a site which was surrounded by watercourses and contained within holy groves. The reliefs from the gateway leading from the court to the hypostyle hall are distributed in museums throughout the world. They consist of long picture sequences depicting the *Heb-Sed* festival for the renewal of kingship of King Osorkon II (924–909 B.C.). In the inner sanctuary of the Temple of Bastet, in a broad, open court, stood seven monolithic naoi, shrines with cult statues of the gods. The architectural remains at Bubastis also include a palace from the Middle Kingdom (c. 1800 B.C.) and a temple complex from Dynasty VI (c. 2300 B.C.).

Bubastis was originally a complex of several square kilometres in area, and to gain an impression of what it may have looked like, it is necessary to visit the ruins at Tanis, about 75 km to the north-east. Tanis, in the far north-eastern corner of the Nile Delta, was the site chosen in 1070 B.C. for the new capital city of the recently independent northern half of Egypt. The ruins of Tanis can be seen on a hill above the salt flats at one of the estuary mouths of the Nile – a good strategic and transport location. Measured from north to south they extend for a distance of 1.5 km.

The main temple of Tanis, dedicated to the god Amun-Re, is the Lower Egyptian counterpart to Karnak, both in terms of theological and architectural significance. It underlined the equality of status of the kings of Tanis with the kings of Upper Egypt in Thebes. This main temple stands on a temple site of 370 x 430 m in area and for its construction the nearby city of Ramesses was used as a quarry. Hundreds of monolithic granite columns, architraves, wall blocks, statues and sphinxes of colossal size were transported the 22 km to Tanis.

The omnipresence of the name of Ramesses II on the monuments of Tanis was until recent decades taken as proof for Tanis being the town of Ramesses. However, research has now shown that at least some of the colossal statues found in Ramesses II's capital, the largest of which weighed about 1 000 tons and was almost 30 m high, were brought from other sites, where they had been placed half a millennium before, during the Middle Kingdom.

One of the original locations for these statues, which include some of the largest ever created in Egypt, was probably Bubastis, especially in view of the ease of trans-

Figure of a ram-god with shrine
This little ram figure is part of the treasure from the tomb of the "Foremost Archer" and Chief Priest, Wenw-djebaw-n-djedet in Tanis. Made of lapis lazuli and mounted in gold leaf, this figure is accompanied by a miniature naos. On the walls of the naos is a relief picture of the divine image. Third Intermediate Period, Dynasty XXI, c. 950 B.C.; gold, lapis lazuli; Cairo, Egyptian Museum

Statue of King Osorkon I
By transferring the royal residence to the Nile Delta, the north of Egypt gained in political significance from the Ramesside period onwards, and also became a centre of artistic activity. King Osorkon had building work carried out in several towns in the Delta. From Byblos; Third Intermediate Period, Dynasty XXII, c. 900 B.C.; granite; Paris, Musée du Louvre

Relief block in Bubastis

The glory of the once enormous temple city of Bubastis, the "town of Bastet", the cat-goddess, can now only be imagined from the descriptions written by the Greek historian Herodotus. Large blocks have survived from one of the temple gates – that of King Osorkon II. The gate's reliefs, now scattered throughout the world, show the *Heb-Sed* festivities which took place to celebrate the renewal of kingship.
Third Intermediate Period, Dynasty XXII, c. 880 B.C.

The ruins of Bubastis

At the edge of the city of Zagazig in the eastern Delta is an extensive site with the ruins of the ancient city of Bubastis, whose buildings dated back to the Old Kingdom.

From the many granite blocks it is possible to reconstruct a temple of Ramesses II, to which belong several of the statues lying at the site.

port from there to Tanis, along an arm of the Nile. Another pointer is that in the ruins of Bubastis fragments of colossal statues of kings have been found that date from the Middle Kingdom.

In the last decade the remains of the city of Ramesses have been excavated; all that is left are a few layers of brick, but it is enough to be able to discern the outlines of stables and armouries, indicating the garrison of the royal residence. However, this capital city of Egypt, now irrevocably destroyed, rises again in the written accounts that were used as reading material in Egyptian schools since the death of Ramesses II and which can give us an impression of what has now been lost to view: "His majesty has built a castle for himself. It lies between Palestine and Egypt. It is similar to Thebes and it endures as long as Memphis. In its western part is the Temple of Amun and in its southern part is the Temple of Seth; the Temple of Astarte is on the morning side and the temple of Uto on the north side. The fortress which is in its interior is like the horizon of the sky."

All these temples were transported away to Tanis to be recombined there in new buildings. At the main gate of the not yet systematically excavated Temple of Amun in Tanis stand colossal Middle Kingdom statues, re-used first in the city of Ramesses II; in the court between the second and third pylons was a veritable museum of sphinxes from the Middle Kingdom, on which are written the names of Ramesses II, his successor Merenptah and King Psusennes I of Tanis. A total of twenty-three obelisks from the New Kingdom have been excavated in Tanis. Although now the Temple of Amun-Re is surrounded by small hills containing the debris of later settlement, when it was built it stood, Acropolis-like, at the highest point of the town and visible for miles across the flat Nile Delta.

Page 173

Temple of Amun in Tanis
In the stoneless Delta the building material for the new residence and its temples was taken from nearby towns which had temples that were no longer important. In particular, the city of Ramesses, just 20 km to the south, was used as a quarry. Also found in Tanis are blocks bearing names of kings from the Old and Middle Kingdoms.
Third Intermediate Period, Dynasty XXII, c. ninth century B.C.

Temple of Amun in Tanis
In the far north-east of the Delta, on a large *tell*, are the ruins of Tanis, the city which became the capital of the northern part of Egypt in about 1075 B.C. Upper Egypt was ruled from Thebes. As a kind of lower Egyptian Thebes, the temples in Tanis competed in size and splendour with those in Karnak.
Third Intermediate Period, Dynasty XXII, c. ninth century B.C.

Gate of the Temple of Amun in Tanis
The colossal statues placed in front of the gate of King Shoshenq bear the name of Ramesses II, but some of them date back to the Middle Kingdom. Ramesses also used statues made in previous periods to give added splendour to his capital city. It is thought that these colossal figures, which would have been transplanted several times, originally stood in Heliopolis or Bubastis.
Third Intermediate Period, Dynasty XXII, ninth century B.C.

At Tanis are also temple complexes for the Near Eastern goddess Anat, the gods Khonsu and Horus, and also, in the outer court of the Temple of Amun, the royal tombs of the rulers in Tanis. Royal tombs in the temple court are also found in Memphis in the same period, and are found again for consorts of the gods in Dynasty XXV in Medinet Habu and are mentioned by Herodotus for kings of Dynasty XXVI in Sais. In addition to the simple underground chambers made of re-used granite blocks, there were also probably burial chapels above ground, but no trace of these structures is now evident. The excavations of the royal tombs in Tanis, discovered in 1939, have produced one of the most valuable treasures ever to have been retrieved from the soil of Egypt, second only to that of Tutankhamun. The finds are now exhibited in the Egyptian Museum in Cairo.

Maned sphinx of King Amenemhat III
By equipping the Temple of Amun in Tanis with statues from earlier periods, it was virtually turned into an open-air museum. The monumental maned sphinxes from the late Twelfth Dynasty bear the names of Ramesses II, Merenptah and of Psusennes, giving evidence of their multiple re-use. The last-named user, Psusennes, placed himself in the context of a long historical tradition.
Middle Kingdom, Dynasty XII, c. 1800 B.C.; Cairo, Egyptian Museum

Temple of Amun in Tanis
No less than twenty-three obelisks have been found in the Temple of Amun in Tanis. They bear the name of Ramesses II and thus give the impression that the temple was built during the reign of this great king – this may well have been the political intention of the kings of the Third Intermediate Period.
Third Intermediate Period, Dynasty XXII, ninth century B.C.

Page 177 above
Ruins of the temple of Behbeit el-Hagar
The most impressive ruins in the Delta are those of Behbeit el-Hagar near to the city of Mansura. Much still remains of the Temple of Isis, built in the fourth century B.C., but probably destroyed later by an earthquake. A reconstruction of the temple would seem quite feasible.
The Late Period, Dynasty XXX, 380–343 B.C.

Shrine to the gods in Mendes
This isolated shrine at the highest point of the ruins of Mendes is all that is left of four that originally stood here in a temple to the ram-god. At 8 m high these monolithic granite shrines are an impressive relic from this important Late-Period town in the Central Delta.
Late Period, Dynasty XXVI, c. 550 B.C.

Mendes and Behbeit el-Hagar

The transfer of the capital city of the pharaohs' empire to the eastern Delta, carried out in the Ramesside period from 1300 B.C. onwards, shows the increasing political and economic importance of the north of Egypt. With the exception of the Nubian Kushites, all subsequent dynasties down to the Ptolemaic period ruled the Nile valley from the Delta.

In their heyday in the first millennium B.C. the main cities of Lower Egypt were by no means inferior to the historical metropolises of Thebes and Memphis. However, we are left today with very few aids for reconstructing their former glory and size. The most complete picture was presented in a travel account by the Greek historian, Herodotus, who spent several months in Egypt between 450 and 440 B.C. and recorded eye-witness accounts of all the important cities in the Delta. Nowadays these sites are a sorry picture, consisting merely of piles of debris which have been sorted and resorted over the centuries.

Sais, in the north-west of the Delta, was the capital of Dynasty XXVI and even at the beginning of the nineteenth century A.D. it still presented a most impressive and extensive landscape of ruins. Herodotus wrote about the shrine of Osiris and the Temple of Neith with its royal tombs; he was full of wonder for the monolithic, 10-m long naos of rose granite brought from Elephantine to Sais by 2000 transport workers.

Not far from Sais is Buto, which has been a religious centre in Egypt since prehistoric times. Herodotus described the sanctuary in the temple of the goddess Uto in the following words: "Its entire height and length is made from a single stone, and all the walls are from that stone, each forty cubits."

Although such travel reports may sound rather exaggerated at first, they are in fact being confirmed by archaeological finds in one of the main towns in the central Delta, in Mendes, the capital city of Egypt in Dynasty XXIX. All that remains of its 400 x 700 m temple area is one of the original four impressive monolithic granite

Relief portrait of King Taharka in Edfu
In Upper Egypt there are few traces of building work from the Late Period. The kings of Dynasty XXV built in Karnak, but in Edfu, too, the remains of a temple from this time have been found under the court of the Ptolemaic Temple of Horus. The head of King Taharka (690–664 B.C.) shows the excellent quality of the relief decoration in this shrine.

The walls of the Temple of Isis in
Behbeit el-Hagar are decorated
with reliefs. These differ from the
sandstone reliefs in Upper Egyptian temples in their material, red
and grey granite, and in the fine
quality of the sculpture.
The Late Period, Dynasty XXX,
c. 380–343 B.C.

shrines, 8 m high, standing on a hill. As in Bubastis and Buto the shrines were placed
in an open court, thus mirroring a typical feature of the sun temples of Dynasty V in
Abu Ghurab and of the Amarna period. In Mendes, too, the royal tombs are located
within the temple area, as in Tanis. The ancient town, still with some well preserved
houses, towers up out of two giant mountains of debris, under which are also concealed a necropolis of the Old Kingdom, and which give an impression of the scale
of what lies beneath.

The desolate condition and the endless dimensions of the ruined sites of these
towns have so far daunted archaeologists. Only in one place is the lost glory and size
of the Delta towns in the Late Period of Ancient Egypt still to be seen, and that is in
Behbeit el-Hagar, near to the city of Mansura in the eastern Delta. Piled up in a
mountain of black and red granite, basalt and quartzite are column drums and hollow cornices, stair steps and blocks with reliefs and inscriptions of the highest
craftsmanship and artistic quality. They form part of the Iseum, the temple to Isis in
Hebet, erected in Dynasty XXX (380–343 B.C.), which was similar in architectural
form to the Temple of Hathor in Dendera. Although some of the relief blocks are today scattered among the world's museums, the building material still on site is comprehensive enough to make a reconstruction of the temple of Behbeit el-Hagar
quite feasible. It is thought that an earthquake was the cause of its destruction.

Individual finds of architectural components and statues at many other places in
the Delta indicate the presence of countless other towns and deliver the archaeological proof for the statements in Ancient Egyptian, Greek, Latin and Arabic texts,
in which the Delta was described as the busiest and richest part of Egypt.

After the New Kingdom the Nile valley between Memphis and Elephantine, from
Cairo to Aswan, became much less important than the Delta. Although extensions
and renovations were indeed carried out on the temples of Thebes, and also on additional smaller temples built there, the main interest of the pharaohs of the Third
Intermediate Period and the Late Period lay in the north.

Thus the architectural achievements of the first half of the first millennium B.C. in Upper Egypt were not in temple-building, but in the development of new types of private tombs. In Dynasties XXV and XXVI, between 700 and 550 B.C., important people, such as the Theban governors under the Kushite and Saite kings, had enormous tombs built for themselves in the Assasif valley, which lay in front of the terrace temple of Queen Hatshepsut (tombs of Montemhet, Harwa, Anch-Hor, Pabasa, Petamenopet and Ibi).

Ideas were taken from the architecture of temples and royal tombs; above ground large brick pylons marked the entrance to the tomb, while the actual sar-

Tomb of Montemhet in West Thebes
The most amazing architectural achievements of the Late Period in Upper Egypt are the tombs of high-ranking people in the Theban necropolis. They lie at the foot of the mountains with the tombs from the New Kingdom, in front of the temples of Deir el-Bahari. Above ground they are marked by brick ramparts and a brick pylon. The actual tomb is below ground. The most significant architectural part is a shaft-like court through which sunlight could penetrate into the underworld.
The Late Period, Dynasty XXVI, c. 650 B.C.

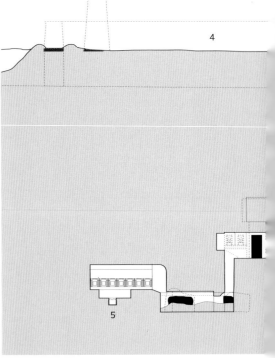

cophagus itself was reached via steps and shafts in the various underground levels leading to the burial chamber.

A new architectural device was open light-wells reached by steps; light could penetrate down them deep into the underworld, whose image is the grave. At the rear of these light-wells was a false door leading to the burial chamber, a motif found as far back as the Old Kingdom, demonstrating the continuing strength of tradition in Ancient Egyptian architecture.

Tomb architecture in the enormous burial complexes of the Late Period in Thebes was not the only area in which forms were used from earlier periods – the same archaic tendencies are evident in reliefs and inscriptions. In part these were simply direct copies from tombs and temples of the Middle and New Kingdoms. The style is in some cases such a perfect imitation of models from centuries or even millennia before that it is almost impossible to distinguish the one from the other.

An additional major influence on the art of this time, around 700–600 B.C., can be seen in the Nubian art of the Kushite kings of Dynasty XXV. These kings ruled Egypt for a hundred years. Two building types are typical of Kushite architecture: the kiosk placed in front of the temple entrance, such as is found on all four sides of the area of the Temple of Amun in Karnak, and the barque station placed in the columned hall. The African component in Kushite art is seen especially in the style of the reliefs, which show the king, and all other persons, as athletic figures with short necks, full lips and low brows.

The contact between Egyptian and Kushite art not only had an effect in Egypt, but also, after the end of Dynasty XXV, began to be felt in the homeland of the Kushites, in Upper Nubia and in the Sudan. The empires of Napata and Meroe, following on from that of the Kushites, drew continued inspiration from this century of close contact with the Egypt of the pharaohs and carried the richness of the Egyptian cultural heritage further up the Nile to the Sixth Cataract, near to present-day Khartoum.

Section through the tomb of Montemhet

The underground chambers of the great Theban tombs from the Late Period extend over several levels downwards to the sarcophagus chamber. Their architecture is reminiscent of the underground tombs of the New Kingdom. Most of these tombs are still awaiting complete excavation and investigation.
1. Pylon
2. Entrance
3. Light-well
4. Tomb of Osiris
5. Tomb chamber

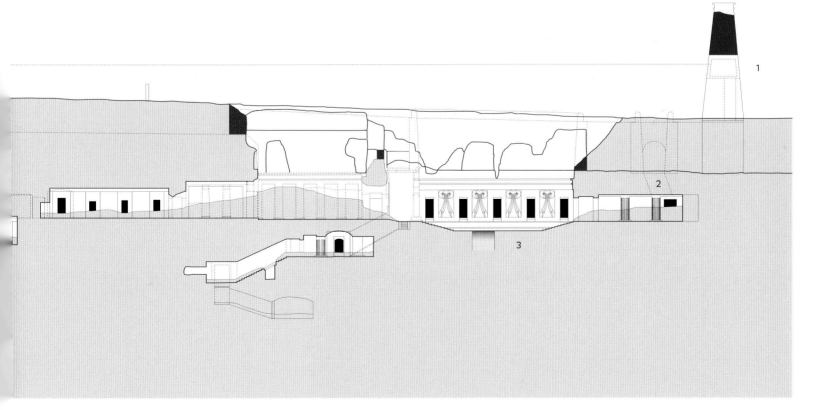

Pyramids and Temples in the Sudan

In the third millennium B.C. the southern border of Ancient Egypt lay at the First Cataract, to the south of Aswan. At the beginning of the second millennium, during the Middle Kingdom, it was extended to the Second Cataract and secured by building fortresses as a bulwark against the serious threat from Egypt's immediate neighbour at the time, the Kingdom of Kerma, centred around the Third Cataract. The New Kingdom extended the territory under Egyptian rule down to Napata at the Fourth Cataract. The Lower Nubian temples of Ramesses II underline this claim to dominance, as do the temples of Amenhotep III in Soleb and Sedeinga above the Third Cataract, and the shrines of Tuthmosis III at Gebel Barkal, near to the Fourth Cataract. In terms of overall plan and iconography these New Kingdom temples on the upper Nile adhere to the generally accepted rules of Egyptian architecture, yet in terms of style they show signs of their special position outside Egypt proper. The colossal statues of Ramesses II in the temple of Garf Hussein, and the ones on the façade of both temples of Abu Simbel, are more compact in their proportions than the figures in Egyptian temples. The papyrus-bundle columns in the temple of Amenhotep III in Soleb are shorter and wider than the pillars of the same type and from the same time in the Temple of Luxor.

The unique artistic style of the Nubian-Sudanese Nile valley did not, however, come to full expression until the region gained political independence when the local royal house in Napata extended its influence beyond the Nubian-Egyptian border to the north and brought the whole of Egypt under its rule in about 760 B.C. These Nubians, called Kushites, after the Ancient Egyptian word "ÔKush" for Nubia, adopted the form of the pyramid for their royal tombs. It was a form that had

Pyramid site of Nuri (Sudan)
During their rule over Egypt the kings of Dynasty XXV, a Sudanese line, did not engage in a great deal of building activity. In their home country, however, they erected royal tombs modelled on the Egyptian style. These pyramid tombs represented a revival of a style which in Egypt itself had died out a thousand years before. Beginning with King Taharka (690–664 B.C.) the Sudanese kings of Napata were buried in Nuri for the next three and a half centuries.

already been abandoned for royal tombs in Egypt at the end of the Middle Kingdom and the Second Intermediate Period, and replaced with tombs cut into the rock. The model for the renaissance of the pyramid style was, however, not the Old and Middle Kingdom necropolis in Memphis. Typically Sudanese pyramids have a 70° inclination, and seldom reach more than 20 to 25 m in height. Both of these features, small format and steep sides, are found in the pyramids above private tombs of the New Kingdom in the Theban necropolis. Thebes, as a centre for the cult of the goddess Mut, consort of Amun and most revered protector of the Kushite king, was most probably the source of inspiration for the Sudanese royal pyramid style, as were also the burial pyramids in Deir el-Medinah, in Gurna and in Dira ` abu el-Naga. The Sudanese royal tombs differ from their Egyptian forerunners both in their cult buildings and in the type of burial chamber. Built on to the east side of the pyramid is a sacrificial chamber, a small, mostly one-roomed mortuary temple. The sarcophagus chamber is hewn in the rock under the pyramid, and reached by a sloping ramp which starts far beyond the east side of the pyramid.

In addition to the formal differences between Egyptian and Sudanese royal pyramids there is also a completely new type of structure for the royal necropolises. In the Old and Middle Kingdoms the individual royal tombs were separate com-

The Great Temple of Amun on Gebel Barkal

Begun under Tuthmosis III around 1450 B.C., the Great Temple of Amun at the foot of the holy mountain was extended under the kings of Napata from the eighth century B.C. onwards. For a thousand years the Gebel Barkal was the religious centre of the Napatan and Meroitic Kingdom, and as such a kind of Sudanese Thebes.

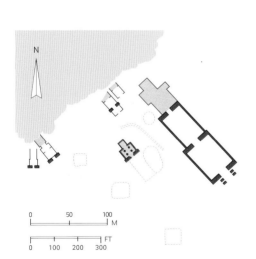

Plan of the temples on Gebel Barkal

The temples of the Napatan kings on the Gebel Barkal were preceded by the buildings of the New Kingdom erected by the Egyptians during the period of colonial rule. Traces of the Nubian Kerma culture (2500–1500 B.C.) on the Gebel Barkal indicate that the oldest temples on the "holy mountain" date back before the New Kingdom.

The royal cemetery of Meroe
At the end of the fourth century
B.C. Meroe became the capital of
the Sudanese kingdom. From
about 270 B.C.–A.D. 320 the kings
and queens of the Meroitic kingdom had their pyramid tombs built
in the desert, on the mountains to
the east of the town, where hundreds of years before members of
the royal family had been buried in
small pyramids. The steep-sided
pyramids reach a maximum height
of about 20 m. On their eastern
side are small temples for sacrificial offerings. The temples each
have an entrance pylon.

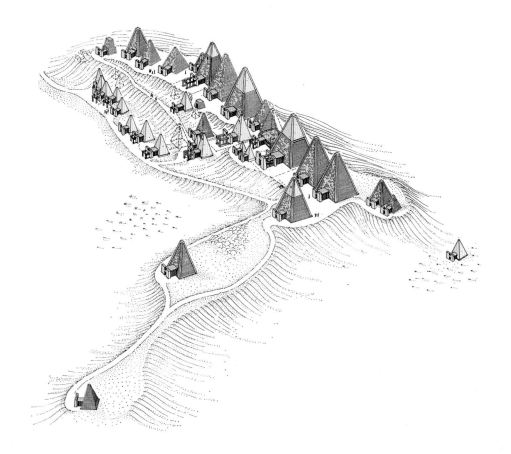

Diagram showing the northern cemetery of Meroe
The pyramids which had been destroyed wilfully in the early nineteenth century A.D. were partly reconstructed between 1970 and 1985 by the German archaeologist Friedrich Hinkel, on behalf of the Sudanese government. This reconstruction shows the original appearance of the northern cemetery, located on a range of dunes high above the Nile valley.

plexes set in broad sites encompassing a valley temple, causeway corridor and mortuary temple, as well as the tombs of other members of the royal family and the royal court.

The Sudanese pyramids, however, are grouped in pyramid sites, and placed very close together, sometimes almost touching. This aspect follows a tradition that reached back before the time of the Kushite dynasty; the tumulus tombs of the chiefs of Napata from pre-Kushite times lie very close together in the cemetery of El Kurru, in which are also buried the founder of the dynasty, King Pye (Piankhy), and other Kushite rulers.

In the Sudan it was less the individual identity of the dead king that determined where he was buried than his membership of a dynasty. The pyramid site of Nuri, just a few kilometres upstream from the capital city of Napata, contains the royal pyramids of all the rulers of the "Napatan" dynasty, following on in about 650 B.C. from the Kushite dynasty. The steep-sided pyramids, including a "bent" pyramid, stand in closely placed rows, one next to the other, together with smaller pyramids of members of the royal family. This arrangement of individual structures as a group is a clear architectural expression of a philosophy of rule in which the tribe, or dynasty, is the focus, and not the individual within it.

The capital city of Napata lay as a kind of political and spiritual centre, half-way between the Kushite royal cemetery in El Kurru and the Napatan royal necropolis in Nuri. Although the actual site of the town of Napata has not yet been located, its size and importance are nevertheless indicated by the temples, lying at the foot of the Gebel Barkal, an impressive table-top mountain dominating the whole surrounding region. This was a mountain that, as the "holy mountain", had been regarded by the kings of Dynasty XVIII, in their conquest of land up to the Fourth Cataract, as a suitable site for a temple to Amun-Re. The temples started by Tuthmosis III (c. 1450 B.C.) were developed in Dynasty XXV into great shrines which followed the Ancient Egyptian sequence of pylons and court, but introduced non-

Pyramid site on Gebel Barkal

The tombs of a few Meroitic kings, around 300 B.C. and 75 B.C., are located on the Gebel Barkal, close to the site of the ancient temples on the holy mountain and not far from the cemeteries of the founders of the Napatan-Meroitic kingdom in El Kurru and Nuri.

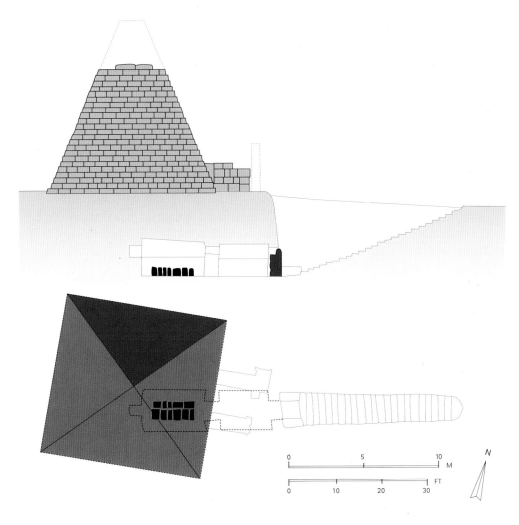

Section and plan of a Meroitic pyramid

A flight of steps leads to the burial chamber of the steep-walled pyramid and to the antechamber under a small temple on the east side. The steps are cut out of rock and start well beyond the pyramid, to the east. The sarcophagus stood on a stone plinth; the approach to the chambers was walled in and the steps covered over after the burial.

Egyptian traditions in terms of their extended linear plan and the kiosks placed in the temple axis. These capital-city temples at Gebel Barkal were decorated with ancient statues from the time of Amenhotep III (c. 1360 B.C.) brought all the way from Soleb; the colossal statues of rams, a motif of the god Amun-Re, which now flank the approach to the largest of the temples at Gebel Barkal, were all dragged from Soleb.

In about 350 B.C. political power shifted from Napata to Meroe, between the Sixth Cataract in the south and the confluence of the Atbara and the Nile in the north. Meroe then remained the centre of the Meroitic kingdom for the next six hundred years. The royal tombs of Meroe lie on higher ground to the east of the town of Meroe. Their form corresponds to that of the steep-sided pyramids in Nuri, and the sacrificial chapels on the east side of the tombs have a pylon as a gate, an idea taken from Egyptian temples. The content of the reliefs on the pylon, showing the enemy being conquered, is also Egyptian in origin.

The reliefs in the offering chambers show a wide variety of themes and individual motifs that are also purely Egyptian: among them are pictures of the deceased at the sacrificial altar, before the judgement of the gods and during the ritual of weighing the heart in the balance. However, the numerous iconographic elements that do not come from Egypt and the quite different style and composition of the reliefs lead us to wonder whether here a new language was being written using the letters of an old alphabet. The unique character and style of Meroitic art is also expressed in the architectural details of the pyramids, the edges of which are emphasised by smooth edging strip and, in the upper part of some pyramids, by roll moulding. The Meroitic pyramids do not end in a pointed tip, but are flattened off and may originally have had sculptural decoration at this point, perhaps a (bronze?) statue of Ba, a bird with a human head, depicting the soul of the deceased. In some pyramids there is a flat niche opening high up on the east side of the shrine, a feature which perhaps led some to believe that treasure chambers were hidden behind these niches. In 1834 many of these pyramids were "beheaded" in an attempt to expose the hidden chambers. Only in one of the pyramids was a valuable treasure found, and that was the gold jewellery of Queen Amanishakhete (c. 20 B.C.), which is now exhibited in museums in Berlin and Munich. As in architecture, the iconography and style of the goldsmiths' work here is quite different to Egyptian jewellery, and represents the creation of a new independent Meroitic style of art using traditional elements.

Pyramids were erected in the royal necropolis in Meroe, first in the south cemetery, later in the north cemetery, over the course of 600 years. Members of the royal family and high dignitaries are buried in very small pyramids in the west cemetery, which lies on the plain between the town and the royal pyramids. In total there are more pyramids in the three burial grounds in Meroe than in the whole of Egypt.

The royal town that was the centre of political power in the Meroitic empire for more than half a millennium has hardly been investigated. Lying between the Nile and the edge of the desert, its Temple of Amun marks the end of a processional street lined by several smaller shrines; this temple, in contrast to Ancient Egyptian tradition, does not face the Nile, but looks east, to where the pyramids of the royal tombs are arrayed along the horizon, an arrangement which again breaks with Egyptian custom, where tombs were located in the west. The giant mountains of debris that mark the site of the ancient town of Meroe are covered with a thick layer of slag-like material, and this has given rise to the belief that there may have been iron-workings in the town. However, we must await further excavations to discover whether Meroe was the ancient world's equivalent of Birmingham.

Although not yet fully investigated archaeologically, there is one other Meroitic town that can give us an insight into the basic forms of Meroitic architecture. This is the ruined town of Naga, to the south-east of Meroe, far from the Nile valley, on a

Shield ring of Queen Amanishakhete
Most of the burial chambers under the Meroitic pyramids were plundered. In only one of them, the pyramid of Queen Amanishakhete, in the northern cemetery of Meroe, did the entire burial treasure remain intact. It was found in 1834 and is today divided between the Egyptian museums in Munich and Berlin. This shield ring shows the ram's head of the god Amun, before a temple façade and encircled by a wide jewelled collar. Roman Period, c. 10 B.C.; gold, glass, carnelian; Munich, Staatliche Sammlung Ägyptischer Kunst

Ram-headed statue from the Temple of Amun in Naga

An avenue lined with twelve ram-headed statues leads to the Temple of Amun. Between each set of front paws is the statue of a king. This type of statue is evidenced 1500 years earlier in the Egyptian temples of the New Kingdom; typically Meroitic, however, is the representation of the sheepskin as spiral curls.
Roman Period, around the time of Christ; sandstone

Temple of Amun in Naga

The layout of the Temple of Amun in Naga, a town in the middle of the desert to the northeast of Khartoum, follows the spatial sequence of Ancient Egyptian temples, from the columned hall through to the inner sanctuary. The relief decoration on the temple gates also follows. The Temple of Amun was built around the time of Christ under the Meroitic King Natakamani and Queen Amanitore.

large site covering more than 1 km². Although its existence has been known about since the beginning of the nineteenth century, little architectural excavation has so far taken place here, yet the town has been preserved almost intact, thanks to its situation far from the major routes of communication. Much of the stone architecture has collapsed, but has remained in piles where it fell, and several temples are still standing. These temples clearly show the three components of the architecture of the Meroitic empire.

In the period of transition the Amun temple was built, with an approach avenue lined with statues of rams, such as had been constructed for the first time almost one and a half thousand years before, linking Karnak with Luxor. The kiosk with its intercolumnar walls, placed in the middle of the avenue of rams, also follows old Pharaonic tradition. The temple itself, with its sequence of gates and halls, is a miniature version of the great classical shrines in the Nile valley in Egypt. Perhaps the small temple to the right of the avenue can also be compared with Ancient Egyptian temple plans and interpreted as a *mammisi*, or birth house.

King Natakamani, who ordered the construction of the Temple of Amun in Naga, also built the Lion Temple there, named after its chief god, the lion (or merely lion-headed) god Apedemak. The front elevation follows classical Egyptian tradition in temple façades: the temple gate is placed between two pylon towers. The large-format reliefs on the front of the pylons show the traditional motif of the king threatening his enemies. A significant feature of Meroitic art is found in the relief decoration of the right-hand pylon tower: it shows, not the king in a threatening pose, but the queen, indicating the dominance of the queen and the queen mother in the Meroitic kingdom. Behind the pylon is a single temple room, the roof of which was supported on four columns. Relief decoration covers all the walls. This type of "one-room temple" is not typical of Egyptian architecture but is a local form, one that can be found in several places in the Sudan, for example in Musawwarat el-Sufra, not far from Naga.

A third component added to these two types of temples is the Hellenistic element. It can be seen in several temple ground plans that follow the schemes laid

Northern pylon tower of the Lion Temple in Naga
The traditional Egyptian motif of vanquishing enemies as a programmatic threatening gesture of the pharaohs is found everywhere on the façades of Meroitic temples and shrines. An unusual feature of Meroitic art is that in this motif Queen Amanitore is also shown as a conqueror of enemies. Roman Period, around the time of Christ

Lion Temple in Naga
The Lion Temple in Naga, dedicated to the Meroitic god Apedemak, depicted either with a lion's body or with a lion's head, contains an element of Egyptian temple architecture in its double-towered pylon. The temple itself consists of only one room, with a wooden roof held up on four pillars. The shrine to the god stood on a stone base. These "one-room temples" are an architectural form characteristic of the Meroitic Empire.
Roman Period, around the time of Christ

Kiosk in Naga

In addition to the Egyptian and the Meroitic architectural influence in the Temple of Amun and the Lion Temple, a third element, the Hellenistic-Roman style, can also be seen in the temples in Naga. This kiosk in Naga, with its capitals and round arches over the windows, is the southernmost example of the influence of Alexandrine architecture. It dates from around A.D. 300.

down in the peripteros and dipteros type of Greek architecture, with a single or double ring of columns surrounding the actual temple building. Ancient Egyptian, Meroitic and Hellenistic formal languages are not merely found to co-exist in Naga, they are mingled within individual buildings. The kiosk of Naga, probably built in the third century A.D., is Egyptian in ground plan and has parallels with the Trajan's kiosk in Philae and with the ones on the roof of the Temple of Hathor in Dendera. The round-arch windows, however, have no parallel in Pharaonic architecture and can only have come from Hellenistic-Roman architecture. Typical Meroitic motifs are interwoven in the details of the architectural ornament.

The kiosk of Naga is the southernmost example of Hellenistic-Roman art. The link established by the Meroitic empire with the Roman world to the north is matched by an equivalent link that is beginning to show itself. Clear analogies are emerging between Meroitic art and the art of the contemporary culture in Nok, on the area now known as Nigeria, which was continued in the sculptures of the Yoruba and in Benin. This points to clear cross-links with Central and West Africa, evidencing an east-west axis of influence in addition to the north-south axis, with the empire of Meroe at the centre. To what extent architecture can be drawn into this framework of influences cannot as yet be established, because of the lack of architectural research in Nigeria.

Egyptian art, whose origins in the fifth and fourth millennia B.C. lay partly in the African continent, returned, at the end of its uniquely long and continuous history, to its roots.

LATE FLOWERING

Temples of the Ptolemaic and Roman Period in Upper Egypt

Page 191

Statue of a falcon in the Temple of Horus in Edfu

Pictorial and architectural styles dating back thousands of years reached perfection in the temples of the Ptolemaic period. The falcon as the god of the skies and the protective deity of the king is as old as the empire of the pharaohs. And here, in one of the latest temples of Ancient Egypt, the Temple of Horus in Edfu, the dignity of this divine animal continues undiminished. Ptolemaic Period, c. 100 B.C.; granite

Relief representation of the goddess Hathor

The over-rich jewellery, the ample figures and the soft, rounded facial features are indications that the reliefs were completed towards the final period of Egyptian art under Roman rule. This representation of the goddess Hathor appears on the outside of the south wall of the birth house in the temple complex of Dendera, which was decorated with reliefs and inscriptions between A.D. 90 and 120. The formal basis for this kind of representation has remained unchanged for 3000 years. It combines front and profile views in a cubist design to produce an image which is unrealistic, but nevertheless complete.

The Temple of Horus in Edfu

When the world-famous temples of Edfu and Dendera, Kom Ombo and Philae are held up as representative examples of Ancient Egyptian temple architecture, then we may wonder, particularly in view of their date of construction, just how it is possible to see in them the essence of 3000 years of continuous architectural history. For none of these temples, as we see them today, was built before the third century B.C.; all belong to a time when the Macedonian Ptolemaic dynasty (304–30 B.C.) and the Roman emperors (30 B.C.–A.D. 395) occupied the pharaoh's throne as foreign rulers.

Despite their late construction date (in Egyptian terms), these temples are nevertheless typical examples of the temple architecture of Ancient Egypt, both in terms of architectonic structure and individual architectural forms. They are bound up in a continuity which encompassed all aspects of life in Ancient Egypt, one determined ultimately by the Nile valley environment, and for which we can still see much evidence today. These later temples of Egypt are extremely well preserved, due in part to their relatively young age of just over 2000 years, and the overall impression conveyed by their courts, halls, corridors and sanctuaries must be very close to that intended when they were first built. It was these same temples which inspired the illustrators of the *Description de l'Egypte*, the publication produced after Napoleon's Egyptian campaign, to fill the hypostyle halls with priests and cult ceremonies.

Today visitors can still descend into the dark underground crypts, climb up to the sun-baked roofs and sky-high pylons, and experience these temples as functioning organisms. The relief pictures and inscriptions, covering not only all inside and outside wall surfaces but also the columns and ceilings, hold the key to understanding the theology and cult ceremonies of such shrines. However, it is a key which can only be used by those who not only master the highly complicated system of the latest stage of hieroglyph writing, with its thousands of symbols, but who also know the code for deciphering this systematically constructed, but very complex, pictographic writing.

The Temple of Horus in Edfu, built between 237 and 71 B.C. on the site of a ruined Ramesside building, is very well preserved and can be used to illustrate the individual architectural components of a Ptolemaic and Roman temple.

Since the days of the Old Kingdom the function of an Egyptian temple was to depict the divine order of the cosmos. The two pylon towers can be seen as the image of the horizon, from which the sun rises; even in the sun temples of Amarna this idea was already quite clear, and on the pylon of the Temple of Horus in Edfu it is represented pictorially. This cosmological symbolism is supported and put in concrete terms by placing the function of the pharaoh within that world order: the front of the pylons carry a representation of the king, holding a sword aloft in a threatening gesture to the enemies of Egypt, in order to subjugate them before the god standing in front of him.

The court behind the pylon represents the architectural link between earth and heaven. The colonnade encircling the court has plant motifs in the column bases and capitals, depicting the vegetation shooting forth from the fertile Nile valley upwards towards the sun. Both the column shafts and the walls behind the ring of columns are covered in frieze reliefs and hieroglyphic inscriptions. The themes in the picture fields seem at first glance to be rather uniform; they show the pharaoh making an offering to the gods. However, iconographic and inscription details show that each individual picture has a specific function, whether that of depicting a particular phase of the cult ceremony, or as part of a geographical system that includes the whole of Egypt in the theology of the temple. The relief pictures fill the court, as the architectural model of the world-view, with life.

From the court narrow openings on both sides of the pronaos lead to an ambulatory surrounding the temple, like a deep, dark ditch, between the doorless and windowless encircling wall and the outer walls of the temple building, protecting it

Pronaos of the Temple of Horus in Edfu

The transition from the light-flooded court to the secret dark interior of the innermost temple rooms is formed by the pronaos, whose half-height intercolumnar front wall nevertheless still enables light to penetrate. The interrupted door lintel also underlines the opening of the pronaos towards the outside. As the room heights decrease inside, this is mirrored on the outside by the falling level of the roofs in the roof court. Ptolemaic Period, c. 237–71 B.C.

Pylon of the Temple of Horus in Edfu

The basic design of Egyptian temple façades remained essentially unchanged for thousands of years. The two pylon towers with the fixing points for the flagpoles, the large-format relief pictures of the king, before Horus and Hathor, setting out to conquer his enemies, and the monumental sculptural decoration had already appeared in the temple façades of the New Kingdom.
Ptolemaic Period, c. 237–71 B.C.

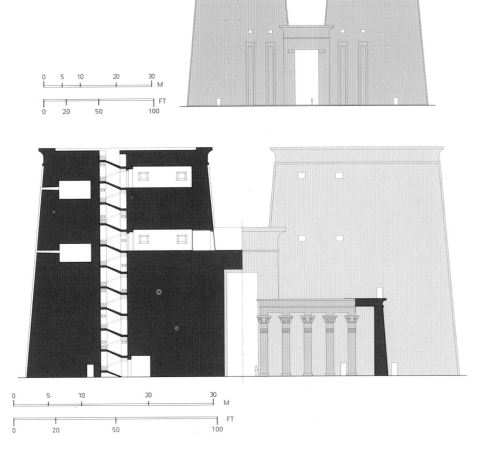

Elevation and section of the pylon of the Temple of Horus in Edfu

Inside the pylons are rooms which were used to give access to the flagpoles. These rooms were reached via a staircase.

like an insulating layer against the outside world. A horizontal band of inscriptions with very large hieroglyphs runs along the base of the outer wall from one side of the temple to the other. It contains a kind of record of the construction of the temple of Edfu, and contains the following information on Ptolemy IX (c. 110 B.C.), who ordered the building of the temple: "He found the temple as a work of his fathers like the horizon of Horus, who is at the top of the sky. The two fronts of the antechamber are carried by lotus and papyrus columns, and it is as splendid as the great palace. He constructed an outer court and a pylon with its gate, he protects its surroundings with this wall on all four sides, following to the book of the order of a temple, drawn up by the High Priest and teacher, Imhotep, the Great One, son of the god Ptah. He made a court with columns along its side and a pylon, reaching to the skies. He surrounded its ambulatory on all four sides with a wall of firm light sandstone, and in this kept to the plan that was begun by his forefathers and as set out in the great plan in this book, that fell from heaven to the north of Memphis."

The history and the architectural form of the temple of Edfu are bound up in a tradition that stretches back over millennia, as far back as Imhotep, the architect of the Step Pyramid of King Djoser in Saqqara. This awareness of tradition on the part of the later builders in Egypt is again expressed in a picture field in the ambulatory: Imhotep is here once more named and represented as a ritual leader in a staged presentation of the Horus myth told in a long series of pictures and text on the outer western wall of the ambulatory.

Court of the Temple of Horus in Edfu
The floral capitals of the columns indicate the origins of the form of Egyptian columns in nature. The sky, supported by the plant columns, spans the court like a roof – an impressive combination of architecture and cosmos. Ptolemaic Period, c. 237–71 B.C.

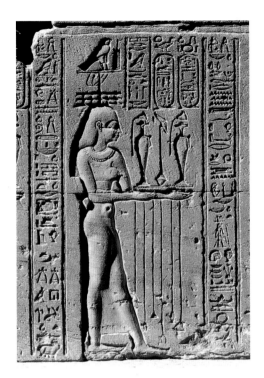

Relief figure showing the personification of a district

Since the Old Kingdom the bases of walls in Egyptian temples had been decorated with reliefs showing long processions of bisexual or female figures who are personifications of the districts or towns of Egypt. They bring offerings from the Nile valley – water, plants and all kinds of animals – as sacrifices to the gods, and thus signify the material basis of life. Ptolemaic Period, c. 237–71 B.C.

Ambulatory around the Temple of Horus in Edfu

The ambulatory between outer wall and temple building is in the form of a deep trench, presenting a barrier between the secular and the sacred. Its defensive role is underlined by the lion-headed water spouts which, according to their inscriptions, ward off storms and rain and all evil things. Ptolemaic Period, c. 237–71 B.C.

Returning to the court, the visitor enters the pronaos in the temple axis. The front of the pronaos consists of columns and, in the same way as in the court colonnade, the general impression intended by the mix of ancient palmiform capitals and typical Ptolemaic, composite floral capitals, is a unified one, a kind of resumé of the wide span of thousands of years of creative activity.

Intercolumnar walls are placed between the pillars of the pronaos front – these are probably the stone representation of carpets hanging in front of the temple façade. They screen the inside of the temple from the court, but allow daylight to enter into this part of the temple, which represents the transition from the secular to the sacred. Before crossing this threshold even the king, as high priest, had first to undergo certain rites. The intercolumnar walls show pictures of the cleansing of the king before he entered the temple, a ritual carried out by the gods Horus and Thoth.

The roof over the pronaos, supported on eighteen columns with composite, floral capitals, bears relief pictures of the starry sky and thus translates the structure of the open court into architectural form. The rear wall of the pronaos is

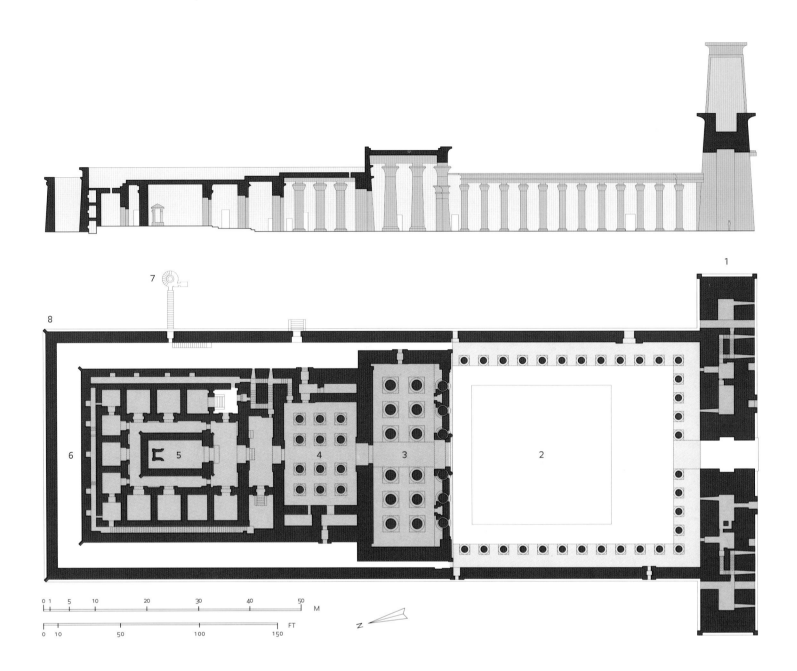

constructed like a pylon tower with sloping sides, roll moulding and cavetto cornice, and thus indicates a tent-like structure placed in front of the actual temple building. So the whole can be seen to imitate its ancient prototypes.

Through the columned hall, the sacrificial altar and the Hall of the Ennead, is the sanctuary, in which stands the shrine with a statue of the god Horus – in Edfu this shrine originally came from an older temple, with inscriptions from the time of King Nectanebo II (c. 350 B.C.). Around the sanctuary, which seems to stand as an independent structure in a larger space, are chapels to other gods. From the court to the sanctuary the floor level rises from room to room, and the room height decreases at the same rate, so that the rising floor level and the falling skyline meet at the point where the image of the god is placed; access to this secret, dark place, away from the brightness of the court, was reserved for the king or a high priest representing him, for the performance of the daily ritual of the cult image.

From the outside, looking from the pylon to the temple, this gradual reduction in height can be seen in the stepped roof, which is not visible from ground level outside the temple, because of the high outer walls. This area on the roof of the temple, under the open skies, played an important part in cult ceremonies and therefore steps were built leading to it from ground level.

Section and plan of the Temple of Horus in Edfu

As the level of the floor rises from the court to the inner sanctuary the height of the rooms decreases, such that in theory the line of the floor rising from the earth to the skies joins up in the inner sanctuary with the line falling from the skies to the earth. The world of humans and that of the gods therefore come into direct contact at this point.

1. Pylon, 2. Court, 3. Pronaos, 4. Columned hall, 5. Inner sanctuary with naos, 6. Ambulatory, 7. Nilometer, 8. Encircling wall

Columns in the court of the Temple of Horus in Edfu

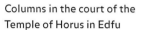

Not only the floral capitals reveal the inspiration from nature, but also the bases of the columns. A stylised ring of leaves twines around the base of the column, showing it as a stem rising out of the round stone base as if out of a mound of earth.
Ptolemaic Period, c. 237–71 B.C.

Coronation of the King

Nekhbet of Elkab, with the Upper Egyptian crown, and Uto of Buto, with the crown of Lower Egypt, as goddesses of the two halves of Egypt, perform the coronation of the pharaoh. His crown unites the two styles of crown in a double crown. Crowned by the gods, the ruler is now their earthly representative and the one who carries out the daily ritual in the temple, as a model of the world.
Temple of Horus in Edfu; Ptolemaic Period, c. 150 B.C.

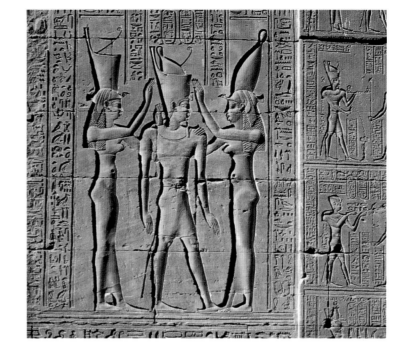

Page 200

Pronaos of the Temple of Horus in Edfu
The closeness of the plant columns in the pronaos does not give the impression of a room, but of a stone forest. The form of the capitals varies from column to column, reflecting the variety in nature, and above them is the stone roof which, with its depiction of astronomical features, represents the sky.
Ptolemaic Period, c. 237–71 B.C.

Sanctuary in the Temple of Horus
The sanctuary is placed almost like a separate volume in the innermost section of the temple. The home for the image of the god is a sacred shrine encased within the multiple layers of temple architecture. The only light in the room enters through openings in the roof, the beams of sunlight piercing the darkness to illuminate the space and the once brightly coloured relief decorations on the walls.
Ptolemaic Period, c. 237–71 B.C.

Now that the inscriptions and reliefs in the Horus temple in Edfu have been made accessible, in publications covering nearly a hundred years of research, the difficult task can begin of translating them and evaluating the content of the entire picture and text programme of the temple, which focused on the myth of Horus. The elemental conflict between good and evil is represented in the battle between the god Horus and Seth, who killed his brother Osiris, Horus's father. The triumphant victory of the youthful hero, Horus, is the mythical expression of the role of the Egyptian king as a guarantor of political and cosmic order, for the pharaoh sits on the "Horus throne". From the earliest times, the pharaoh bore the name Horus as the first of his names; he was the earthly form of god.

The ancient surroundings of the temple of Horus lie under 10 to 15 m of the debris of later occupation, on part of which the modern town of Edfu stands. In the course of millennia the town grew up around the temple and finally covered it entirely. It was not until the excavation work in the nineteenth and twentieth centuries that the temple was again brought to light – almost undamaged, apart from the systematic hacking off of faces, hands and feet from all the representations of people. This was carried out by early Christians, eager to destroy the work of heathens and to convert Ancient Egyptian shrines into Christian churches, a process that can be seen in many other places.

Inner room of the sanctuary in the Temple of Horus in Edfu
The inside of the innermost sanctuary is completely dark. Only during the daily ritual of the cult image does daylight penetrate to the shrine and the altar block on which the god's barque could be placed. From inside this place of quiet and sanctity, the outside world seems far away, kept at a distance by the succession of temple rooms, courts and perimeter walls.
Ptolemaic Period, c. 237–71 B.C.

Shrine to the gods in the Temple of Horus in Edfu

The king as high priest (or the high priest representing the king) processed from the secular outside world to the sacred inner sanctuary along a long path to perform the ritual of the cult image, at the shrine with the god's statue. This shrine, which actually comes from an older temple, was the most precious part of the whole complex. It bears the name of Nectanebo II (c. 350 B.C.) and is made from a granite monolith. Inside it was a small shrine of gold in which the golden statue of the god was kept.

In excavating the temple a small shrine was found close by, to the left of the main temple axis. In its position in relation to the main temple, its architectural type and its pictorial programme, this temple is very similar to the birth houses in Dendera. This shrine or birth house is the place in which Horus and his goddess Hathor celebrated the divine marriage, and from which the youthful god Harsomtus emerges, "Horus, who unites the two lands"; in other words, a divinity closely related to the king. The myth of the divine birth of the Egyptian king, as evidenced in the temple in Luxor for Amenhotep III and in Deir el-Bahari for Hatshepsut, is translated here into divine spheres.

In its alignment parallel to the south-north course of the Nile, the Temple of Horus in Edfu breaks the basic rules for placement of Ancient Egyptian temples, which were usually positioned at right angles to the Nile, but in its clarity of ground plan it is nevertheless the classic example of a "house of god".

The Temple of Isis on Philae

A very individual and unusual temple complex from the Ptolemaic-Roman period, quite unlike that in Edfu, is situated in the far north of Nubia at the beginning of the First Cataract, on the Nile island of Philae. Here, at the border between Kushite tribal land and Egypt proper, King Taharqa (690–664 B.C.) of Dynasty XXV built a shrine to the god Amun, perhaps as a kind of religious and political interface between the two regions. Under Amasis (570–526 B.C.) the first Temple of Isis was built on Philae, and many hundreds of the relief blocks used in its construction have survived.

The history of the temple complex we see today began with Nectanebo I (380–362 B.C.) who built a kiosk on the southern tip of the island. To the north of the kiosk he built a temple gate and a hundred years later this gate was integrated in the First Pylon of the Temple of Isis. From that time onwards, into the period of the Roman emperors, many individual temples were constructed all over the island, their location probably determined by the rocky terrain. This is also an explanation for the irregular plan of the Temple of Isis; a giant lump of granite was reformed into a stele and used where it stood in the right-hand tower of the Second Pylon.

The outer court of the Temple of Isis extends in a trapezium shape from the kiosk of Nectanebo towards the First Pylon, thus gaining optical depth. The steps, flanked by lion statues and leading to the First Pylon, are a very un-Egyptian building form, which can perhaps be explained by the need here to accommodate the steeply sloping granite terrain. The temple axis changes direction twice, and, for reasons of lack of space, the birth house, which should lie at a right angle to the axis, in front of the temple, is placed here instead between the First and Second Pylons and is turned into the temple axis.

The Temple of Isis on the island of Philae

The great temples of the Ptolemaic Period in Upper Egypt were built as far south as Philae. This island on the Nile, just south of the First Cataract, in fact lies beyond the borders of Egypt, in the far north of the Nubian Nile valley. As a result of this location the temples on Philae were virtually predestined to be the model for temples built further to the south, between the First and the Second Cataracts, during the Ptolemaic-Roman Period. Philae's influence can even be seen much further to the south in the Meroitic Kingdom.
Ptolemaic and Roman Period, c. 250 B.C.–third century A.D.

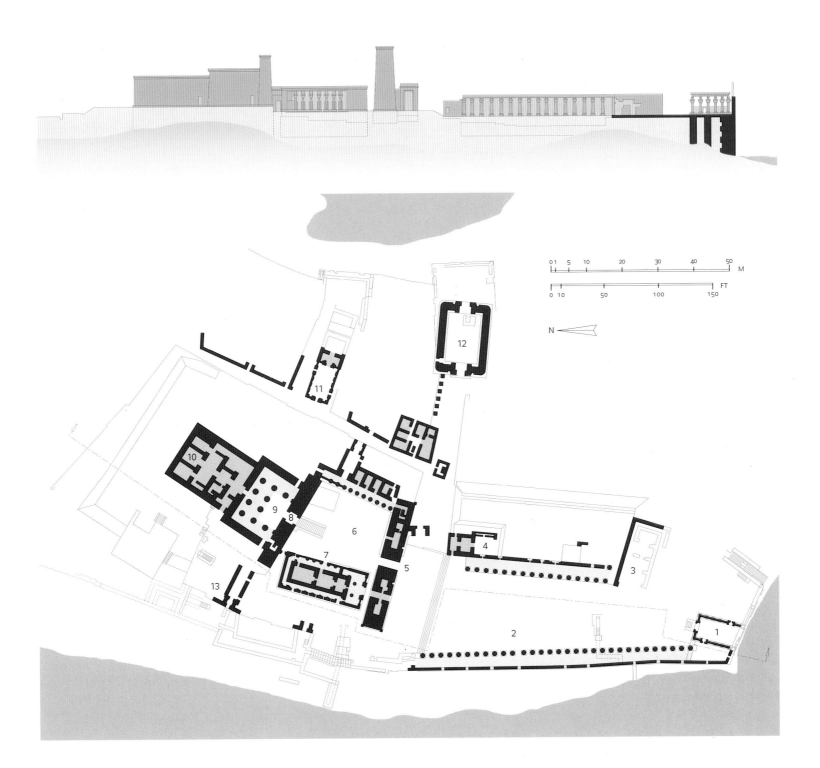

Elevation (from the west) and plan of the temples on Philae

The axis of the Temple of Isis is angled a number of times along its length from the kiosk on the southern tip of the island to the inner sanctuary. The ancillary temple structures are also arranged irregularly. The reason for this unusual layout probably lies in the problems posed by the topography of the island and its granite cliffs. The birth house, which should normally be placed in front of the temple at a right angle to it, is found here parallel to the axis, between the first and the second pylons. Also, the changes of level between the outer court and the inner temple zone are here more clearly marked than in other temples. Again the topography is thought to have been the determining factor.

1. Kiosk of Dynasty XXX
2. Outer court with colonnades
3. Temple of Arensnuphis
4. Chapel of Imhotep
5. First pylon
6. Court
7. Birth house
8. Second pylon
9. Columned hall
10. Inner sanctuary
11. Temple of Hathor
12. Roman kiosk
13. Hadrian's gate

West colonnade of the outer court of the Temple of Isis on Philae
The outer court in front of the first pylon in the Temple of Isis is unusually long and narrow. Its left-hand, western colonnade stands on the inside of a court wall which falls away steeply towards the Nile. The changing shapes of the plant capitals create the impression that the court, as an island in the Nile, is surrounded by a papyrus thicket. Roman Period, first century A.D.

According to the classical model of the Temple of Horus in Edfu, behind the Second Pylon should be a columned court, the pronaos with its intercolumnar walls and the hypostyle hall. However, in the Temple of Isis, lack of available building space has led to an original compression of the plan. The court has shrunk to 5 m in depth, and the colonnades on both sides consist of only a single column. Immediately behind the intercolumnar walls of the pronaos façade is the hypostyle hall with just one row of columns.

In this compact enclosure stands the Temple of Isis like a fortress of the gods at a point on the Nile that has been of the greatest importance for the whole of Egypt since ancient times. The First Cataract was thought to be the source of the Nile; it was here, from the rapids around the granite cliffs of the cataracts, that the river flowed into Egypt, at Elephantine. The god of creation worshipped on the island of

Capital at Trajan's kiosk on Philae

The 2500-year-old motif of the papyrus column developed in the composite columns of the Ptolemaic Period into a bundle of papyrus plants, built up from the bottom of the column to the top in layers of increasing thickness.
Roman Period, c. A.D. 100

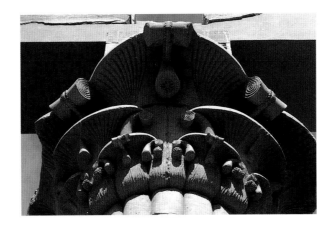

First Pylon of the Temple of Isis on the island of Philae

The sharp difference in levels between the court and the pylon, created by the lie of the land, also prompted the use of a flight of steps, in a way quite untypical of Egyptian temples. Also unusual is the door in the pylon tower on the left; normally two statues of gods would stand here, as seen in front of the pylon tower on the right. The door leads to the birth house directly behind the pylon. The central door arch in the pylon dates from Dynasty XXX; the pylon towers were added later, during the Ptolemaic Period.

Page 209
Birth house in the Temple of Isis on Philae
The birth house stands like an independent architectural unit on the western edge of the court between the first and second pylons of the Temple of Isis. Placed around the actual temple structure is a ring of columns with composite and Hathor capitals, supporting the roof like a shade-giving canopy. Between the columns are half-height inter-columnar walls which are meant to screen from view the inside of the temple, the birth-place of the divine child.
Ptolemaic and Roman Period, c. 250 B.C.–third century A.D.

Capital on the birth house of the Temple of Isis on Philae
The shape of the columns is appropriate to the function of the birth house, i.e. as a place in which the goddess-mother gives birth to her divine offspring. The capital shows the head of the goddess Hathor. In this human features are combined with the ears of a cow, thus indicating the animal form of the goddess of the skies.
Ptolemaic and Roman Period, c. 250 B.C.–third century A.D.

Elephantine is Khnum, who formed mankind on his potter's wheel. In front of his temple is the "Nilometer", the measuring mark on which the leaner and the fatter years of life in the valley can be read off. The idea of the First Cataract as the source of the Nile is illustrated in a temple relief on the island of Philae: the Nile god Hapi, in human form, is depicted crouching in a rocky cave and pouring water out of a container.

During the last few centuries before Christ the island of Philae and its temples formed the border between Ptolemaic Egypt and the independent kingdom of Meroe. Since the conquest of Egypt by Rome this was also the southern border of the Roman Empire; various attempts by the Roman emperors to extend their territory further south failed. The position of the island as a border-post of the Empire also explains the upsurge in building activity in the first and second centuries A.D. Under Emperor Augustus the colonnades of the large outer court and a small Temple of Hathor were built; under Trajan, the grand kiosk on the eastern edge of the island was constructed; and under Hadrian and Marcus Aurelius, a monumental gate was built to the north-east. A considerable portion of the reliefs and inscriptions in the entire temple area were executed in the period of Roman rule.

Columned hall of the Temple of Isis on Philae
This idealised view, painted by the artists who accompanied Napoleon's Egyptian expedition, makes the columned hall of the Temple of Isis on Philae seem much wider than was ctually the case in the narrow confines between the second pylon and the inner zone. The colourful wall and column reliefs, however, give an authentic impression of the hall and its spatial effect.
After: *Description de l'Egypte,* 1809

Columned hall in the Temple of Isis
The lack of suitably broad, flat expanses on which to build led on Philae to a fusion of pronaos and columned hall. Behind the second pylon is a court which has only one row of columns, followed by the columned hall with only two rows of columns, separated off from the courtyard by intercolumnar walls. Ptolemaic and Roman Period, c. 250 B.C.–third century A.D.

Cult activities on the island of Philae continued into the sixth century A.D.; the latest hieroglyphic texts (A.D. 394) are to be found on Philae, and so, too, the latest demotic inscriptions (A.D. 452), and as such the last dated example of a script that originated three and a half thousand years before. The particular tenacity of Ancient Egyptian religion on the island is due certainly to its border location; Philae became an island retreat for believers in the old gods, an escape from advancing Christendom.

For Egypt's southern neighbours, Nubia and the Sudan, Philae played a multiplier role in terms of relaying Egyptian religion, script and art up the Nile for hundreds of years. Several small temples in Lower Nubia have reliefs which are direct parallels to the Temple of Isis on Philae, and even in more distant places, like Musawwarat el-Sufra and Meroe in the Sudan, the influence of the texts in the Temple of Isis can be seen in the hieroglyphic inscriptions in temples and tombs.

On Philae itself the gods of Meroe are not only present in the wall reliefs but also have shrines dedicated to them. The god Mandulis has a chapel in the east colonnade, and, in about 210 B.C., in a prominent place just behind the entrance kiosk, a temple was built to the Meroitic god Arensnuphis.

Representation of the source of the Nile

An unusual picture on Hadrian's Gate to the west of the second pylon of the Temple of Isis on Philae shows the Nile emerging from its source at the First Cataract. A plump Nile god wearing a head-dress of papyrus leaves squats in a cave under the high granite cliffs of the First Cataract. In his hands he holds containers from which flows water. He is thus presented as the source of the life-giving water. Roman Period, second century A.D.

No less than four Christian churches were built on the island, from the middle of the sixth century A.D. onwards, as a counterbalance to the bulwark of Ancient Egyptian religion which survived on Philae longer than anywhere else.

The special role played by the temples on Philae continues even today. As part of a UNESCO campaign to rescue the ancient buildings of Nubia now under threat from the Nasser Dam, these temples were the last to be moved in their entirety to a higher location on the artificially enlarged island of Agilkia. The monuments on Philae had already suffered severe damage from the beginning of the twentieth century, after the construction and raising of the old Aswan dam, which resulted in the island being under water for at least part of the year. The dismantling of the temples and their reconstruction on a safe site has not only saved these "pearls of Egypt" with their much lauded harmony of architecture and landscape, for later generations, but have also provided a valuable opportunity to investigate the older structures concealed beneath the Ptolemaic temples. It was this archaeological work which uncovered the Kushite origins of the temples of Philae.

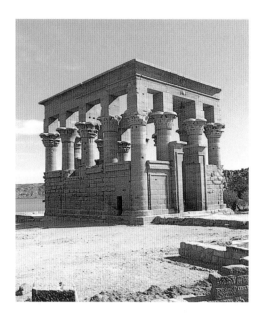

Trajan's kiosk on the island of Philae

The last monumental building in the temple complex on Philae is a kiosk for processions of the gods. The kiosk was begun in about A.D. 100 but was never finished. There are almost no reliefs or inscriptions apart from a few preliminary drawings and secondary texts. As in the case of other kiosks there was no solid stone ceiling, just a wooden construction to support a tent-like covering.

Trajan's kiosk on the island of Philae

Many thin plant stems are bound together into massive columns with capitals shaped into variously sized umbels. The high header blocks above the composite capitals were probably intended to be decorated with Hathor heads, as in the birth house. Above the doorway on the cavetto are two rough blocks, one above the other, to which sun discs with uraeuses would have been attached.
Roman Period, c. A.D. 100

The Temple of Hathor in Dendera

Many temples bear the traces of a transformation from Ancient Egyptian shrine to Christian church. In the festival hall of Tuthmosis III in the Temple of Amun in Karnak paintings of Christian saints overlay the column reliefs. The inner courts of the mortuary temple of Ramesses III in Medinet Habu were converted into closed church rooms. The term nowadays used for the mortuary temple of Hatshepsut, "Deir el-Bahari", means simply "north cloister", indicating that Coptic monks built a cloister in the ruins of the Pharaonic shrine.

These later changes to Ancient Egyptian building structures have largely been obliterated in the course of archaeological excavations to uncover the original, older buildings. However, the interweaving of temple and church can still be seen to this day in the complex of the Temple of Hathor in Dendera. Without destroying, or even damaging, the shrines to the old gods, a church was built right in front of the façade of the pronaos on the west side of the outer court.

Despite the late date of its construction – started in the late Ptolemaic period, then continued under Tiberius and Nero, but never fully completed – the whole Hathor Temple complex is the best preserved example of a late Egyptian temple complex. A channel was dug at a right angle from the Nile to the temple, thus establishing the temple's axis. Encircling the temple area of 280 x 280 m is a mud-brick wall, 10 m thick. The alternating concave and convex curved segments of the wall show a clear wave structure, which is probably intended as an image of the primordial sea out of which the temple rises as a primordial hill, a place of creation.

Reconstruction of the temple complex of the goddess Hathor in Dendera
The temple precinct of the goddess Hathor in Dendera has survived very well, due to its late construction date (54 B.C.– A.D. 60). Inside the encircling wall, on the right in front of the Temple, are the birth houses and the "sanatorium"; in the back right-hand corner of the temple is the sacred lake and, behind the temple, a shrine to the goddess Isis. A few hundred metres away to the south-east is a separate temple precinct to the god Harsomtus. The Temple of Hathor was never completed. Only rudimentary stone foundations were laid for the pylon and the inner perimeter wall.

Church in the outer court of the Temple of Hathor in Dendera
In the late fifth century A.D. a Christian church was built between the two birth houses on the right-hand side of the outer court of the Temple of Hathor. The Ancient Egyptian temples were left intact. The sacred sites of the older Egyptian and the newer Christian religion stand side by side in peace and harmony.

Within this enclosure and to the right of the temple is a well preserved holy "lake", which is a 25 x 30 m basin walled with sandstone blocks. It was used for cult purposes, such as ritual boat journeys and cult games, and was a mythical place and source of holy water. Not far from this pool, on the west side of the outer court, is a brick building with small walled basins in its large inner court; around the court are small cubicles. Inscriptions state that the function of this building was a place of healing, or sanatorium, where patients were treated by means of a series of baths, healing sleep and magical practices. Two other temples are situated on the same side of the outer court at right angles to the axis of Temple of Hathor, but separated from each other by the church erected at a later date; the temples have similar ground plans, but are in different states of preservation – the older one, built under Nectanebo I (380–362 B.C.), has been largely destroyed, while the more recent one, from the time of the Emperor Trajan (A.D. 98–117), is almost fully preserved. The temple building itself is surrounded by an ambulatory of plant columns with composite capitals, of which the abacuses are decorated with relief figures of the god Bes. The function of the building is indicated by the architectural type, Bes motifs and the reliefs on the intercolumnar walls showing Hathor and her young son Harsomtus; the relief cycles inside the temple elaborate upon this theme. Amun-Re and Hathor enter into a divine marriage, from which union results Harsomtus, "Horus, who unites the two lands". The birth house, a fixed component of temple complexes in the Ptolemaic-Roman period, is a stone version of a tent roof supported on plant columns, in the shade of which the mother, segregated from the

Façade of the pronaos of the Temple of Hathor in Dendera
As the pylon was not completed the main front is formed by the pronaos, which should actually have been the back wall of the temple court. The column form, with its Hathor capitals, is a direct reference to the divinity to whom the shrine is dedicated.
Roman Period, c. first century A.D.

Sacred lake in the temple complex of Dendera
The sacred lake is an integral part of an Ancient Egyptian temple complex. It had quite a varied role in the day-to-day life of the temple – as an image of the primeval ocean, as a stage for ceremonial boat trips and as a reservoir for water. On all four sides of this very well preserved lake basin in Dendera we can still see the steps which led down to the bottom of the lake.

Relief at the Temple of Hathor in Dendera

The Roman emperor, as a pharaoh, makes a sacrifice to the goddess Isis and her son, Harsomtus. This son, "Horus, who united the two lands", is the original divine image of the king. The linking of rulers and religion continued into the Late Period in Egypt. From an Egyptian point of view, even the foreign rulers, Ptolemaic and Roman, were holders of the high office of pharaoh, without which the world order could not be maintained.
Roman Period, c. 54 B.C.–A.D. 60

Roman birth house in Dendera

Both the decoration of the header blocks above the composite capitals with figures of the god Bes, and the relief pictures on the intercolumnar walls refer to the cult function of the temple, as the place in which the divine marriage between Amun and Hathor and the birth of their child Ihy was celebrated. The cult role of the king bringing sacrifices to the gods is fulfilled by the ruler, even though this ruler is now a Roman emperor.
Roman Period, c. 54 B.C.–A.D. 60

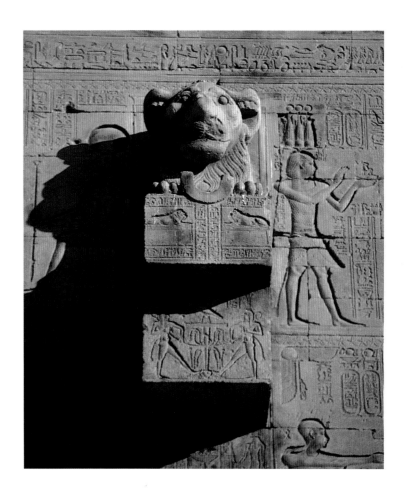

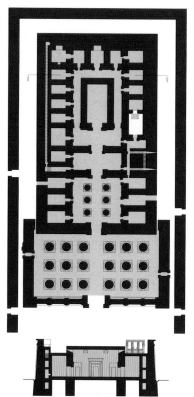

Page 218 above left

Water spout at the Temple of Hathor in Dendera

Water channels cut through the temple walls drain water from the roof courtyard above the inner temple rooms and direct it through an opening between the front paws of the lion-shaped spouts. The inscription describes the lion as a creature that wards off evil and protects the temple from bad weather.
Roman Period, c. 54 B.C.–A.D. 60

Page 218 above right

Plan and cross-section of the Temple of Hathor in Dendera

The ground plan of the temple differs little from the standard layout of Ptolemaic temples. The succession of pronaos, columned hall, sacrificial hall, hall of appearances and inner sanctuary is almost identical with that of Edfu. The cross-section shows the three levels of crypts concealed within the outer walls.

Page 218 below

West side of the Temple of Hathor in Dendera

Only the water spouts indicate the level of the roof court above the inner rooms of the temple. This court is hidden from view behind the outer wall, which is extended upwards. The sloping sides and shaped cornice are reminiscent of the origins of stone architecture in mud-brick building.
Roman Period, c. 54 B.C.–A.D. 60

Pronaos of the Temple of Hathor in Dendera

The sistrum columns, typical of Dendera, bear the face of Hathor on all four sides of the capitals. The stranded wig framing the woman's face and cow-ears of each Hathor head is at the same time a very skilful solution for a smooth transition at the corners.
Roman Period, c. 54 B.C.–A.D. 60

main building, passes her confinement, protected by the gnome-like god Bes. However, a divine marriage also links Hathor of Dendera with Horus of Edfu, the product of which union is Ihy. As god of music he embodies an essential characteristic of his mother Hathor, as expressed in the iconography of her shrines and in particular in her temple in Dendera: the columns of the pronaos, the front of which now forms the façade of the temple (because the court and pylon were never finished) are in the form of monumental sistra or rattles. Above the column shaft the capital is in the form of a four-sided Hathor head, a woman's face seen from the front, with cow's ears, alluding to the animal form of the mother goddess. On top of the capital, again on all four sides, is depicted the façade of a chapel, flanked by cow's horns stylised into spirals. In the hypostyle hall these complex capital forms sit on top of another, composite capital, thus reducing the shaft length to only half that of the column.

The Hathor-head motif, so characteristic of the temple façade, is met again on a larger scale on the rear external wall of the temple building. Here it takes the form of a very deeply cut relief, placed exactly on the temple axis, half-way up the wall. Surrounding the Hathor head we can see dowel holes which would have been used for fixing gold sheet panels, and also fixing points for a small chapel used as a popular place of devotion; this would have been a kind of mirror image of the shrine itself. On the other side of this wall, at exactly the same spot in the central axis of the temple, is a small Hathor head, placed on the back wall of a temple space on the upper floor, where the cult image of Hathor was probably kept. The inner sanctuary could thus be projected to the outside through the temple walls without itself being subjected to the gaze of the common people.

The key events in an Egyptian temple, the encounter between the king and the image of god, always remained shrouded in secrecy. The brick ramparts protect the

Roof of the pronaos in the Temple of Hathor in Dendera
The roof and the architrave are decorated with representations of the path of the sun, thus turning the stone temple roof into an image of the heavens. Here in Dendera, the skies are not supported by plant columns but by monumental Hathor sistra, rattles used in the cult of the goddess. The architecture thus becomes a visible and immediate symbol of cult music in honour of Hathor. Roman Period, c. 54 B.C. – A.D. 60

Sanctuary in the Temple of Hathor in Dendera

The pictures of the path of the sun on the ceiling of the pronaos are matched in the innermost room of the temple, in which the sanctuary stands like a separate building, with small openings in the roof and at the top of the walls. During the course of the day these openings allow the sun to track across the reliefs on the outer wall of the sanctuary, bringing this star into the picture world of the temple walls.

Roman Period, c. 54 B.C.–A.D. 60

Wall relief in the pronaos of the Temple of Hathor in Dendera

The wall reliefs of Ptolemaic temples are generally divided into a series of small scenes. A closer study of the pictures and the hieroglyphic inscriptions reveals a detailed and very well thought out system of theological, cult and topographical references in which each picture has a carefully worked out place.

Roman Period, c. 54 B.C.–A.D. 60

temple area from the outside world and the encircling wall conceals the actual temple – in Dendera this wall did not pass the foundation stage and is therefore particularly easy to recognise. The outer wall of the temple building is continued upwards behind the pronaos to such a height that it transforms the roof space above the temple rooms into a broad enclosed court. In this space are several small shrines of great cult significance. In a kiosk with Hathor columns the union of the cult statue Hathor with the sun-god was celebrated, and in the two chapels of Osiris cult ceremonies of the resurrection of the murdered god took place as part of the Osiris mysteries. Apotropaic, lion-headed gargoyles pierce the outer wall of the temple roof to keep evil away from the important cult area.

Equally invisible from the outside are the crypts of Dendera, laid out in a corridor system on three floors inside the massive outer walls of the temple. The exceptionally carefully worked wall reliefs tell the secret of the function of these inaccessible spaces, reached only through hidden hatches; they were the treasuries in which the golden cult objects of the temple were kept. In the texts in the crypts the foundation of the Temple of Hathor is traced back to the time of the Old Kingdom. Three thousand years of religious and artistic tradition have found lasting expression here.

The Victims of Progress: Temples Destroyed in the Nineteenth Century

All the large temples from the Ptolemaic-Roman period follow the same rules governing overall structure. The sequence of spaces, from pylons to the inner sanctuary, is an essential feature, and fulfils cult requirements in terms of the temple serving both as the place where man and god meet in the daily cult image ritual and as a representation of the cosmos through the themes depicted on the walls and ceilings. In all temples the ceilings, with their astronomical representations, are images of the heavens, opening the temple to the sky, and to a certain extent also belying their own architectural substance. The ritual scenes on the walls present, in a fixed sequence of cult proceedings, a compressed and ritualised form of life. The lower part of the walls and the temple flooring embody the floor of the Nile valley, from which the created world rises up in the form of pillars. The temple as a model of the world, an architectural programme valid from the days of the Old Kingdom, is most impressively formulated in the later temples.

Despite this overall scheme for temple architecture, each of the major Egyptian shrines, from the Old Kingdom until the Roman rule, has a quite unique and individual character. The few temple remains we can still see today are just a small number of the many temples built from the First Cataract down to the Mediterranean. In addition to the well preserved temples at Edfu, Philae and Dendera there is also an unusual shrine in Kom Ombo, dedicated to two gods of equal status and featuring, accordingly, two parallel temple axes; in Esna, too, one of the latest Egyptian temples, worked on until A.D. 250, a unique complex, has survived, although only the pronaos is left standing in the Temple of Khnum.

Just two centuries ago, at the time of Napoleon's Egyptian campaign, there were considerably more well-preserved temples than now. To the south of Thebes, as part of the Temple of Montu in Armant, was a birth house from the late Ptolemaic Period with a unique double kiosk in front of its façade. In 1861/62 it was demolished and its sandstone blocks used for building a sugar factory. A similar fate befell several temples in Elkab, a shrine to Thoth, the main temple of Nekhbet and a barque shrine from the time of Tuthmosis III.

Close to Esna, in 1828, the Temple of Isis in Contra Latopolis (c. 100 B.C.–A.D. 180) was destroyed, and in 1843 in the same area the small temple of El Deir was used to provide the building material for a factory in Esna. In Central Egypt, in around 1830, the ruins of the Ptolemaic temple of Antaeopolis were exploited as a quarry, delivering building material for the construction of a palace in Assiut. The list of similar acts of vandalism is much longer, and is not restricted to buildings constructed in the later periods of Ancient Egyptian architecture, but extends to all periods of Pharaonic history. Two shrines of the New Kingdom on the island of Elephantine were no longer in existence in 1837, although they were shown on illustrations from the early part of the nineteenth century as completely preserved structures.

Under Viceroy Muhammed Ali the industrialisation of Egypt had absolute priority above all other interests, and thus, in expectation of development aid benefits, he generously allowed foreign museums to collect Egyptian antiquities. Although nowadays archaeological research has quite different criteria and priorities, we can hardly accuse the archaeologists of

Temple of Montu in Armant
In about 40 B.C., under Cleopatra VII, a temple was erected in Armant to the south of Thebes. No trace of it remains today. Napoleon's archaeologists, however, were still able to see this impressive building. Half a century after their visit the temple was dismantled block by block to provide building material for a nearby sugar factory.
After: *Description de l'Egypte*, 1809

Temples in the town of Elkab

The rectangular-shaped urban district of Elkab in Upper Egypt had a number of New Kingdom temples within its walls. The only impression we can still gain of these buildings comes from early nineteenth-century publications, as the same fate befell these temples as befell the Temple of Montu in Armant.
After: *Description de l'Egypte,* 1809

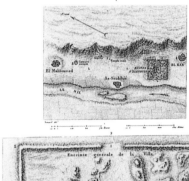

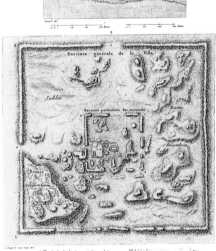

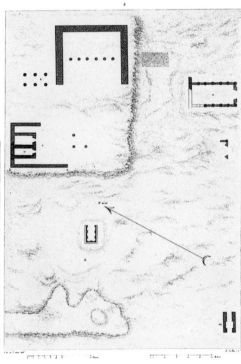

Temple in the El-Kebir district

Man's destruction of the temples in Egypt was aided and abetted by nature. In 1821 the Ptolemaic temple in the El-Kebir district in Central Egypt was swept away and completely destroyed by the Nile floods. The drawings in *Description de l'Egypte* give an impression of how it used to look. All the columns were plant columns.

Temple of Amenhotep III on Elephantine
In 1822 two temples on the island of Elephantine near Aswan were completely destroyed. The temple of Amenhotep III consisted of a two-roomed sanctuary, with a row of pillars on each long side and two columns flanking the entrance. Not far from this spot a temple of Tuthmosis III was also destroyed in the same year.
After: *Description de l'Egypte,* 1809

that time of irresponsibly stripping the country of thousands of antiquities and transporting them away. If it were not for the activities of those museums, the majority of the works they collected would by now have been burned in lime-kilns or incorporated in industrial buildings. A change in Egypt's attitude towards its ancient monuments seems only now to be taking place, less for reasons of historical interest, than out of materialistic concerns; the care of Egypt's ancient monuments has become a very important factor in tourism, which is of key economic significance for the country. However, this new-found motivation in preserving the ancient monuments has been unable to deal with the immediate threat posed to these monuments by environmental pollution and the population explosion.

Temples near Esna
The temples of Contra Latopolis and El-Deir near Esna were dismantled in 1828 and 1843 to provide stone for industrial buildings. The only impression we now have of these Ptolemaic structures is in *Description de l'Egypte,* 1809.

Epilogue

Egyptian Influence in the West

Propylaeum in the Königsplatz in Munich

In classical architecture Ancient Egypt played only a minor role. Greek and Roman influence was so dominant that even when Egyptian models were used, they remained a secondary element. The two pylon towers of the Propylaeum in the Königsplatz in Munich (1846–1860) are overshadowed by the central gateway built in the form of a Doric temple.

At the end of almost three thousand years of history in Ancient Egypt the cultural tradition of the empire of the pharaohs lived longer in its southern sphere of influence than in its Egyptian home. In an Egypt under Roman rule, the formal structures and motifs of Egyptian art faded into the background and became rare phenomena in early Christian art in that country. In architecture there was a direct line of development from the floral capitals of the temples during the Roman period, the Temple of Khnum in Esna being the best example, to the basket capitals of the early churches; these in turn had an indirect influence via Byzantine art on early Romanesque art. In the architecture of early Christian monasteries, which made use of old temples as quarries, certain Ancient Egyptian forms were retained; the outer wall of the White Monastery near Sohag is crowned by a hollow cornice, for example.

Long before its demise, however, Egyptian architecture, as part of Egyptian art, had nevertheless left clear traces beyond the Nile valley. In view of the political and cultural dominance of Egypt in the Eastern Mediterranean, it can be no surprise to find typical Egyptian forms on Cyprus, in architecture dating from the first half of the first millennium B.C. Many Egyptian-style statues and Hathor capitals demonstrate the popular Egyptian style on Cyprus at the time. Carriers of these motifs were Egyptian-style designs on Phoenician ivory carvings. Less well known, perhaps, is the evidence of the influence of Egyptian architecture in the Nabataean rock city of Petra, to the north of Aqaba in present-day Jordan: here we find not only obelisks which were probably modelled on Egyptian examples, but also rock-cut tombs, some of the façades of which are finished with roll moulding and cavettos. Recent evidence of worship of the Egyptian goddess Isis in Petra underlines the links between this city and its Egyptian neighbour.

An exchange of art forms between places that are close to each other is understandable, but the presence of Egyptian elements in the architecture of Rome, so far from Egypt, cannot be explained in terms of geographical proximity. No less than fourteen ancient obelisks stand today in Rome. Their locations are some of the most important squares in the city: St Peter's Square, Piazza del Popolo, Piazza Rotonda in front of the Pantheon, Piazza Navona, the Lateran basilica, Trinità dei Monti above the Spanish Steps and the Quirinal. Originally there were probably more than forty obelisks in Ancient Rome. Many of them were brought to Rome from temples all over Egypt, from Heliopolis to Karnak. In their new location they served partly as trophies, as symbols of the victory of the would-be world power of Rome over the former might of the pharaohs, who submitted to Rome with the suicide of the last of the Ptolemies, Cleopatra. Other obelisks that were erected by the Roman emperors had a quite different function. They were placed in the heart of Ancient Rome, on the Field of Mars, in a temple devoted to the worship of the Egyptian gods, Isis and Sarapis (Osiris-Apis). As far as we can reconstruct from the Forma Urbis, a town plan of ancient Rome, and from the results of the few excavations in this area, the architectural form of this temple has no direct reference to

original Ancient Egyptian architecture, but has instead its own distinct language of forms. However, it was perceived to be typically Egyptian in style, and is found in other places within the context of shrines to Egyptian gods. The semi-circular exedra in the southern part of the Iseum Campense in Rome has a counterpart in Praeneste, where Isis was worshipped from the second century B.C. onwards, and in the Villa Hadriana in Tivoli, the Emperor Hadrian's garden palace with its artificial Nile, a long pool of water along the edges of which were placed statues of Egyptian gods. The shrines of Isis in Rome were a mixture of pseudo-Egyptian architecture, historicising effects with Egyptianising columns and statues and also a real museum containing original obelisks and statues, imported from Egypt.

From these first cult shrines to Egyptian gods in Rome, the worship of Isis, Osiris and Apis spread throughout the entire Roman empire. Thus the death of the Egyp-

Obelisk in the Piazza Navona in Rome

In the days of the Roman Empire, Egyptian monuments were transported to Rome for two reasons – on the one hand as trophies and on the other as prized relics of an ancient and revered culture. Many of the Egyptian objects found in Rome, including several of the fourteen Roman obelisks, originally stood in a temple to the Egyptian gods which was located not far from the Pantheon, on the Field of Mars. The obelisk in the Piazza Navona bears the name of Emperor Domitian (A.D. 81–96), written in hieroglyphs.

tian religion in Egypt coincided with a spread of Egyptian cults through the entire known world at the time.

An upsurge of interest in the culture of the pharaohs, fired by this flowering of Ancient Egyptian tradition far from its place of origin, has been apparent in Central Europe since the Middle Ages. In the thirteenth century Egyptian sphinxes sculpted for the Lateran basilica were doubtless modelled on the ancient ones transported to Rome. In San Marco in Venice the mosaic pictures of the story of Joseph show the grain stores of the pharaohs in the form of steep-sided, pointed pyramids. Reports and probably also drawings by the crusaders, who often made a special trip into Egypt, south to Cairo, may well have been the source of such ideas. The towering height of the pyramids of Giza seems to have made such a lasting impression that it led to an exaggeration of the proportions of pyramids.

The pyramids in the paintings of Nicolas Poussin and in the architecture of J.B. Fischer von Erlach are very similar, in terms of their steeply sloping sides, to the pyramids in Deir el-Medinah and in the Sudan. However, neither Upper Egypt nor even the Sudan were on the route of the early travellers to the East. And so it can only have been their imagination that led to these forms. Hubert Robert, in his fantastic paintings, delivered the proof: the tips of his steep-sided pyramids disappear completely into the clouds.

The rediscovery of the ancient world by Renaissance scholars directed attention to Egypt via the writers of antiquity. Egypt was famed as the cradle of wisdom by both Greeks and Romans, and has ever since in Western tradition become regarded, in widely differing world-views, as the origin of human civilisation. The guiding intellectual forces of the French Revolution looked to Egypt in the same way as the Freemasons; similarly, for Louis-François Cassas and the Prussian King Frederick William II, Egypt was a source of inspiration, as it also was for Friedrich Schinkel and the Bavarian King Ludwig I.

The traces of the architecture of the pharaohs reach down to the present day. The late French president, François Mitterrand, had his monument, the pyramid at the Grand Louvre, built in Pharaonic dimensions and style.

Mosaic in San Marco in Venice
One of the channels through which knowledge about Ancient Egypt has been transmitted to the West is the Bible. The Old Testament story of Joseph and his brothers is sometimes placed firmly in an Egyptian context. The grain stores of the pharaoh, which Joseph so carefully managed, are represented as pyramids in the mosaics of San Marco in Venice (thirteenth century).

Pyramid of Cestius in Rome

In 15 B.C. the praetor C. Cestius had a tomb built in the form of a pyramid. This was not unique in Ancient Rome. At about 35 m in height the Pyramid of Cestius was much higher than the Meroitic kings' pyramids, but had the same angle of inclination.

Pyramid in the "Neuer Garten" in Potsdam

The Prussian King Frederick William II had a French-style ice-cellar built in the shape of a pyramid in the "Neuer Garten" in Potsdam (1791). In the tradition of Freemasonry he saw it as a symbol of Egyptian wisdom.

Glass pyramid of the Louvre in Paris

In postmodern architecture the pyramid shape is enjoying a remarkable renaissance worldwide. The most spectacular example is the glass pyramid which now forms the main entrance to the Grand Louvre in Paris. This pyramid has become a new symbol of the city. J. M. Pei, 1982–1989

CHRONOLOGICAL TABLE

Step Pyramid of King Djoser in Saqqara

Sphinx in Giza

Monuments

4th millennium B.C.
Structure made of wood and mats
3100 Beginnings of brick architecture
The first royal tombs in Abydos
3000 Royal cementery in Abydos
Brick tombs in Saqqara
2800 Funerary temples of brick in
Abydos and Hierakonpolis
First use of stone in building

2650 First monumental stone building:
the Step Pyramid of Djoser in
Saqqara
Small cult pyramids from
Elephantine to the Delta
2600–2550 From the step pyramid to the real
pyramid: Pyramids of Medum and
Dahshour
2500–2465 Peak period of pyramid building:
Pyramids of Cheops, Chephren,
Mycerinus in Giza
2465–2325 Pyramids in Abu Sir
Sun temples in Abu Ghurab
Mastaba tombs with relief decora-
tion during the entire period of the
Old Kingdom
2325–2150 Pyramids in the south of Saqqara
Temples in Heliopolis and Bubastis
Rock tombs in Central and Upper
Egypt

3600–2650 B.C.
Prehistoric and Early Dynastic

2650–2150 B.C.
Old Kingdom

Historical Events

Prehistoric
3600–3300 **Naqada I** – Culture based in Upper
Egypt, influenced by Nubia and the
Sudan
3300–3100 **Naqada II** – Culture in Upper and
Lower Egypt, influenced by the
Near East

Early Dynastic
3100–3000 **Dynasty O.** First kings of all Egypt
3000–2800 **Dynasty I.** Consolidation of the territory of the empire from Aswan to
the Nile Delta. Capital city is
Memphis. Development of a hieroglyphic writing system
2800–2650 **Dynasty II.** Last remaining internal
political unrest settled

2650–2575 **Dynasty III.** State organisation,
religion, script and art fully developed
2575–2465 **Dynasty IV.** Political and cultural
golden age
2465–2325 **Dynasty V.** Empire cult of the sun-
god Re
2325–2150 **Dynasty VI.** Decline in the power of
the pharaohs, regional governors
strive for self-rule

Statue of King Djoser from Saqqara

Statue of King Chephren from Giza

2150–2040 Small royal pyramids in Saqqara
Rock tombs in Central and Upper
Egypt

2040 Terrace temple of King
Mentuhotep II in Deir el-Bahari
(Western Thebes)

c. 2000 Founding of the Temple of Karnak

1950 The "White Chapel" of King
Seostris I in Karnak

2000–1800 Temples built in all towns in the
country
Royal pyramids in Lisht, Dahshour,
El-Lahun, Hawara
Rock tombs in Central Egypt (Beni
Hasan, Meir, Assiut, El-Bershe) and
Upper Egypt (Thebes, Aswan)
Fortifications at the Second
Cataract in Nubia

1550–1070 Royal tombs in the Valley of the
Kings (Western Thebes)
Mortuary temples and Rock tombs
in Western Thebes
Temple of Karnak

1470 Terrace temple of Hatshepsut in
Deir el-Bahari (Western Thebes)

1450 Temple of Tuthmosis III on the
Gebel Barkal in the Sudan

1360 Temple of Amenhotep III in Luxor
and in Soleb (Sudan)

1350 The Aten Temple of Amenhotep IV
in Karnak

1348–1335 Buildings in Amarna

1325 Tomb of Tutankhamun in the Valley
of the Kings (Western Thebes)

1300 Temple of Sethos I in Abydos

1250 Rock temples of Ramesses II in Abu
Simbel (Nubia)
Mortuary temple of Ramesses II in
Western Thebes (Ramesseum)

1150 Mortuary temple of Ramesses III in
Medinet Habu (Western Thebes)

Pylon in the Temple of Luxor

1070–712 Temples and royal tombs of Tanis in
the Delta

2150–1550 B.C.
From the First to the Second Intermediate Period

First Intermediate Period

2150–2040 **Dynasties VII–X.** Short-lived
reigns, some localised

2134–2040 **Dynasty XI.** Theban rulers

Middle Kingdom

2040–1991 **Dynasty XI.** Thebes becomes the
new capital of Egypt

1991–1783 **Dynasty XII.** Egypt becomes one of
the leading powers in the Near
East. Memphis again becomes the
capital city. Thebes becomes the
religious centre

1783–1640 **Dynasties XIII–XIV.** Many short
governments, decline in power

Second Intermediate Period

1640–1532 **Dynasties XV–XVI.** Foreign rule by
the Hyksos from the Near East.
Capital city Avaris in the eastern
Delta

1640–1550 **Dynasty XVII.** Independent Theban
kings

Statue of King Tuthmosis III from
Karnak

1550–1070 B.C.
New Kingdom

1550–1307 **Dynasty XVIII.** Rise of Egypt to
world power. Thebes is the political, religious and cultural centre

1353–1335 **"Amarna period".** Monotheist
reform under King Amenhotep IV-
Akhenaten, foundation of the new
royal residence in Amarna.
Restoration under Tutankhamun
and Horemheb

1307–1196 **Dynasty XIX.** Power politics by the
Ramessides against the Hittites
and the Libyans. Residence in the
eastern Delta

1196–1070 **Dynasty XX.** Threat from mass
migration ("Sea Peoples") and
internal political decline

1070–712 B.C.
Third Intermediate Period

1070–945 **Dynasty XXI.** Division of Egypt into
a northern empire with its capital
in Tanis and a southern empire with
its capital in Thebes

945–712 **Dynasty XXII.** Libyan rule over
Egypt

828–712 **Dynasties XXIII–XXIV.** Collateral
lines lead to internal political col-
lapse

Gold mask of King Psusennes I from
Tanis

Pyramids of the Napatan kings in
Nuri (Sudan)

Hellenistic architecture in Alexandria
Hellenistic towns in the Fayum
Hellenistic necropolis in Tuna el-Gabal
Temples in pure pharaonic tradition

Ptolemaic and Roman Period
250 B.C.–3rd century A.D.
 Temple of Isis on Philae
 237–142 Temple of Horus in Edfu
150 B.C.–A.D. 250
 Temple of Khnum in Esna
150 B.C.–2nd century A.D.
 Temples in Kom Ombo
54 B.C.–A.D. 60
 Temple of Hathor in Dendera
300 B.C.–A.D. 300
 In the Sudan, temple buildings in
 Meroe, Musawwarat el-Sufara and
 Naga
 Royal pyramids in Meroe and at the
 Gebel Barkal

First Pylon of the Isis Temple on
Philae

750–664 Temples at the Gebel Barkal
 (Napata) in the Sudan
 Royal tombs in El Kurru and the
 pyramids of Nuri in the Sudan
 Temple buildings in Karnak
700–600 Large tombs in Assasif (Western
 Thebes)
 500 Temple in the oasis of Kharga
400–350 Temple buildings from the Delta
 (Behbeit el-Hagar) to the First
 Cataract (Philae)

Monuments

750–332 B.C.
The Late Period

332 B.C.–A.D. 395
Ptolemaic and Roman Period

Historical Events

750–664 **Dynasty XXV.** Kushite kings from
 the Sudan rule as pharaohs of
 Egypt. Karnak becomes an outpost
 of the capital city of Napata at the
 Fourth Cataract in the Sudan
664–525 **Dynasty XXVI.** Sais in the Delta
 becomes the capital city of Egypt.
 Successful resistance against the
 Kushites and the Assyrians. A
 period of renaissance
525–404 **Dynasty XXVII.** Egypt under
 Persian rule
404–343 **Dynasties XXVIII–XXX.** The final
 phase of Egyptian independence.
 Capital city in Mendes and
 Sebennytus in the Delta
343–332 **Dynasty XXXI.** Egypt again conquered by the Persians

332–30 Alexander the Great and his suc-
 cessors, the Ptolemaic kings.
 Alexandria becomes the new cap-
 ital. Egypt becomes a part of the
 Hellenistic world. Continuation of
 religious and cultural autonomy in
 Middle and Upper Egypt
30 B.C.–A.D. 395
 Egypt is a part of the Roman
 Empire
395–642 Egypt is a part of the East Roman
 (Byzantine) Empire

Relief of the goddess Hathor in
Dendera

GLOSSARY

Apotropaic: Preventing evil. Lion-headed gargoyles act as apotropaic architectural elements to keep rain and storms away from temples.

Architrave: Stone beam placed horizontally across pillars or columns to support the roof construction over a space.

Barque sanctuary: In Egyptian temples the barque sanctuary is situated in front of the inner sanctuary in which is placed the image of the god. The barque sanctuary contains the god's barque in which the image of the god is carried in processions leading out of the temple.

Book of the Dead: Religious texts written mostly on papyrus. The texts deal with the transfiguration of the deceased.

Cataract: A large waterfall or rapids. The Nile has six cataracts, from the confluence of the Blue and the White Nile in Khartoum to Egypt. The cataracts are impassable for boats.

Causeway: A raised paved pathway connecting the valley temple with the pyramid complex. Mostly with stone walls along the sides and finished with a stone roof construction.

Cavetto: Upper, hollowed member found on the upper part of walls in stone architecture, mostly found in combination with roll moulding.

Cenotaph: An empty tomb designed as a symbolic burial place of the gods (Osiris tomb) or of special beings of the king.

Colonnade: A row of columns, one or two deep, surrounding a court.

Colossal statue: Larger-than-life statues, representing mostly kings and gods, seldom non-royal persons. Placed mostly in public spaces (courts and temple façades).

Column: An architectural support, the form of which in Egyptian architecture is mostly derived from models found in nature. Often carved from a single stone, seldom composed of a number of blocks.

Papyrus column: The imitation in stone of a papyrus stem (single or in a bundle) with typical wedge-shaped cross section.

Papyrus-bundle column: A stone representation of several plant stems bound together. A typical column form under a capital.

Cornice: The upper finish of a wall consisting of roll moulding and cavetto. A typical feature in Egyptian architecture.

Crypt: Passageways built into the walls of temples for storage of cult objects. Often extending over several storeys. Entrances hidden by sliding blocks of stone.

Dynasty: A group of rulers, who, on the basis of family relationships or a shared base for their royal residence, are seen as a single unit in the list of Egyptian Kings. The dynastic divisions were first introduced by Ancient Greek historians and are still adhered to today.

Eight deities, the: A group of eight gods which can personify all gods, in that eight is a double of four, the defined plural.

Ennead: A group of gods, representing all gods; nine being the square of the plural number three.

Exedra: An open space, raised on a podium and open on one side.

Fluting: Vertical surface pattern on columns, probably fashioned to resemble wooden posts.

Hed Sed: The jubilee of kingship, celebrated after 30 years reign. Frequency can vary.

Hemispeos: A temple in which the innermost part at the back is cut into the rock (speos = temple cut into a rock face).

Hieratic: Cursive form of hieroglyphic script, mostly written on papyrus.

Hollow relief: Typical technique for applying pictures and inscriptions to outer walls: the outer limits of the design are marked and the details chiselled out. The background thus stands proud around the representation.

Hypostyle hall: A columned hall, mostly with a raised central nave and lower side aisles. The most important architectural component of temples since the New Kingdom.

Intercolumnar walls: Half-height walls between columns. Often used on the front of pronaoi, or on kiosks and birth houses. Probably originated from the custom of hanging carpets between roof supports.

Kiosk: A free-standing baldachin supported on lightweight pillars. When executed in stone, the roof was generally non-permanent, consisting of strips of tent cloth. Intercolumnar walls between the columns.

Kushites: A dynasty named after Kush, the Ancient Egyptian term for Nubia and the Sudan. They ruled over Egypt from 745—655 from Napata (Fourth Cataract).

Mammisi: "Birth house"; small temple located in front of and to the side of large temple complexes. Regarded as the place in which the mythical birth of the king or god-child took place.

Monolith: A monument hewn from a single block of stone. Obelisks, naoi and colossal statues are always monolithic, columns often are.

Naos: A shrine to a god. Stone naoi stood in the sanctuaries in the temples and served as places to put the divine image.

Necropolis: A city of the dead. The wide areas covered by Ancient Egyptian cemeteries justify the term "city".

Obelisk: A stone pillar, square in cross-section and tapering towards the tip. The tip is shaped like a pyramidion (small pyramid) and was sometimes gilded. Since the Old Kingdom, generally placed in pairs in front of and in temples and in front of tombs as a cult monument to the sun-god.

Ostracon: A potsherd or piece of limestone used for writing exercises in school or for sketches and designs in the sculptor's workshop.

Palettes: Stone plaques in geometric or figural shapes; in prehistory and early history these were used as make-up tablets in tombs or as votive offerings in temples, in the case of the latter often with relief decoration.

Pectoral: A piece of jewellery worn on the breast. Often in the form of a temple façade.

Pharaoh: The Ancient Egyptian name for a king, originally from the word *pr-ò* meaning "great house".

Portico: Column or pillar arrangement at the entrance to a building.

Pronaos: The inner portico in front of the columned hall in the temples since the New Kingdom. Either open to the court, or separated by intercolumnar walls.

Pylon: The entrance gateway to a temple. A pair of towers, rectangular in plan and with slanting walls, flank the actual entrance portal. On the front are insertion points for flagpoles. Inside is a series of steps leading up to the roof of the pylon.

Pyramid: A royal tomb with a square base and four sloping (or, very occasionally, bent), triangular sides meeting at the apex. Typical form of royal tombs in the Old and Middle Kingdoms, also used by the Kushite, Napatan and Meroitic kings of Sudan. In the New Kingdom this form was also used for private tombs.

Bent pyramid: The transition stage between a step pyramid and the real pyramid shape (Dahshour). Seldom found in Sudan (Nuri).

Classical pyramid: A pyramid shape, with sides sloping up at a 52° angle and built on a square ground plan (Giza, Abu Sir).

Step pyramid: The earliest stage of development of the pyramid form. Dates from Dynasty III (Saqqara, Medum).

Pyramid texts: Hieroglyphic texts for the transfiguration of the dead king. Found on the walls of underground rooms in pyramids since the end of Dynasty V.

Roll moulding: A round section carved out of the corner blocks on buildings. The form is derived from the idea of plant stems used to protect the edges in mud brick architecture.

Sanctuary: The inner sanctum. The innermost space in a temple, in which is found the naos and the divine image.

Sarcophagus: From the Greek, meaning "flesh-devouring". A large stone coffin.

Serdab: The Arabic word for "cellar". An inaccessible chamber in the above-ground part of a mastaba in the Old Kingdom. The place in which statues were kept.

Sistrum: Rattle instrument of the goddess Hathor. It consists of a cylindrical shaft, above which is a Janus-faced woman's head with cows ears. Above that is the musical part in a box or bow shape. The sistrum is used as a capital form in Hathor temples and *mammisi*.

Sphinx: A figure having the body of a lion and a human head (rarely, animal heads such as falcons, rams, jackals). Mostly the divine image of a king.

Stele: An upright stone, free-standing or placed against a wall; stelae with inscriptions and relief decoration were used as votive monuments.

Tell: A hill built out of the ruins and debris of successive cultures.

Temple: Temples rate alongside tombs as the most important type of buildings in Egyptian architecture. The house of the gods, cult place for the dead, a world model and mythical place are its key functions.

Mortuary temple: In the Old and Middle Kingdoms this was the place for the cult of the dead in the royal pyramid. The main function of the mortuary temples of the New Kingdom is as a temple to the god Amun.

Terrace temple: Style of temple architecture specific to Thebes (Mentuhotep II, Hatshepsut). The levels rise in terraces from the outer court to the sanctuary.

Valley temple: The entrance structure to a pyramid complex. Situated on the edge of the valley, and linked to the mortuary temple by a causeway corridor.

Tomb: Tombs, as "Houses of Eternity" are an important type of building in Egyptian architecture. They rate alongside temples.

Hall tomb: Large, one-roomed rock-cut tombs (e.g. during the Middle Kingdom).

House-type tomb: A type of tomb structure in which elements from ordinary house architecture have been adopted – eg. sloping side walls, matting and basic layout. This corresponds to the idea of the tomb as a "house for the dead".

Mastaba: The Arabic word for "bank" or "mound"; a description for the above-ground tomb structures, with square ground plan and sloping outer walls. Sometimes solid, sometimes containing many interior rooms and courtyards, which can be entered.

Rock-cut tomb: Underground tombs cut out of solid rock. These tombs range from simple one-chamber structures to extensive sequences of rooms on several levels (King's tombs of the New Kingdom, tombs of the Late Period in Thebes).

Triad: A group of three gods forming a theological unit. One of basic structures of Ancient Egyptian religion.

Umbel: The leaf cluster of the papyrus plant; the basic form of a capital on a papyrus column.

Uraeus: The snake head in the iconography of kings and gods. It is a being that wards off evil and represents various goddesses.

Vault: An arched roof structure made of stone or mud brick.

Included in this bibliography are only the more recent publications which give an overview of the architecture of Ancient Egypt and information about the current status of archaeological research. The specialist literature on the individual subject areas is easily accessible via these publications.

Albouy, Marc, H. Boccon-Gibod, J.-Cl. Golvin etc.: *Karnak – Le temple d'Amon restitué par l'ordinateur,* Paris, 1989.

Arnold, Dieter: *Building in Egypt – Pharaonic stone masonry,* New York, Oxford, 1991.

Arnold, Dieter: *Die Tempel Ägyptens – Götterwohnungen, Kultstätten, Baudenkmäler,* Zurich, 1992.

Arnold, Dieter: *Lexikon der ägyptischen Baukunst,* Munich, Zurich, 1994.

Aufrère, Sydney; J.-Cl. Golvin and J.-Cl. Goyon: *L'Égypte restituée – Sites et temples de haute Égypte,* Paris, 1994.

Aufrère, Sydney; J.-Cl. Golvin and J.-Cl. Goyon: *L'Égypte restituée – Sites et temples des déserts,* Paris, 1994.

Badawy, Alexander: *A history of Egyptian architecture,* 3 vols., Lawrence, Berkeley, Los Angeles, 1954–1968.

De Cenival, Jean-Louis and H. Stierlin: *Ägypten – Das Zeitalter der Pharaonen* (Architektur der Welt), Munich, 1964.

Edwards, I.E.S.: *The pyramids of Egypt,* Harmondsworth, 1985.

Giedion, S.: *Ewige Gegenwart,* Vol. 2, *Der Beginn der Architektur,* Cologne, 1965.

Golvin, Jean-Claude and J.-Cl. Goyon: *Karnak, Ägypten – Anatomie eines Tempels,* Tübingen, 1990.

Golvin, Jean-Claude and Cl. Traunecker: *Du ciel de Thèbes,* Paris, 1983.

Klemm, Rosemarie and D. Klemm: *Steine und Steinbrüche im alten Ägypten,* Berlin, 1993.

Lange, Kurt and M. Hirmer: *Ägypten,* Munich, 1967.

Leclant, Jean (Ed.): *Ägypten,* 3 vols. (Universum der Kunst), Munich, 1979–1981.

Martin, Geoffrey T.: *Auf der Suche nach dem verlorenen Grab,* Mainz, 1995.

Müller, Hans-Wolfgang and S. Lloyd: *Ägypten und Vorderasien* (Weltgeschichte der Architektur), Stuttgart, 1987.

Sauneron, Serge and H. Stierlin: *Die letzten Tempel Ägyptens,* Geneva, 1975.

Smith, W. Stevenson: *The art and architecture of Ancient Egypt.* Revised with additions by William Kelly Simpson (Penguin Books), Harmondsworth, 1981.

Spencer, Jeffrey: *Brick architecture in Ancient Egypt,* Warminster, 1979.

Stadelmann, Rainer: *Die ägyptischen Pyramiden: Vom Ziegelbau zum Weltwunder,* Mainz, 1985.

Stierlin, Henri: *The pharaohs' master-builders,* Paris, 1995.

Stierlin, Henri: *Égypte – Des origines à l'Islam,* Paris, 1984.

Teichmann, Frank: *Der Mensch und sein Tempel,* Ägypten, Stuttgart, 1978.

Uphill, Eric P.: *Egyptian towns and cities* (Shire Egyptology 8), Princes Risborough, 1988.

Vandersleyen, Claude (Ed.): *Das alte Ägypten* (Propyläen Kunstgeschichte 15), Berlin, 1975.

Vandier, Jacques: *Manuel d'archéologie égyptienne,* II/1–2, Paris, 1954–1955.

Wildung, Dietrich: Lehmbau in Ägypten, in: Hans Wichmann (Ed.), *Architektur der Vergänglichkeit – Lehmbauten der Dritten Welt,* Basle, Boston, Stuttgart, 1983.

INDEX – Monuments

ACKNOWLEDGEMENTS AND CREDITS

The author, together with the photographers and the publisher, would like to express their gratitude to the Egyptian Authorities for the facilities provided and permits granted during the various assignments undertaken in Egypt for the preparation of this book.

Their particular thanks go to the Department of Antiquities in Cairo, and to the directors of the Egyptian Museum in Cairo and the Luxor Museum. They are also indebted to the Tourist Information office of the Arab Republic of Egypt for its assistance in this venture.

The author would also like to express his gratitude to the Authorities of the Republic of the Sudan for their kind help during his expeditions to the archaeological sites in their country.

The following documents are from the author's own archives:

Pages: 6, 12, 14 right, 16, 17, below, 19 right, 20 right, 24, 26, 27, 28, 38, 39, 42 above left and below right, 43, 45, 50, 51, 53, 60, 61, 62, 63, 64, 65, 71, 82, 83, 84, 87, 88, 89, 100, 101, 106, 107, 19 below, 112 above, 113 below, 114, 115, 116, 120, above, 121, 122, 124, 125 above, 132 below, 143 below, 145 below, 154, 156 above, 157, 158, 159, 161, 162, 164, 171, 172, 174, 175, 176, 177, 178, 180, 181, 182/183, 185, 186, 187, 188, 189, 211, 215, 225, 227, 228, 229 left and below.

In addition, a series of documents are from the following sources:

Page 173: © Joachim Willeitner, Munich.

Page 23: © Gallimard – L'Univers des Formes, Paris.

Page 85: © Georg Gerster, Zumikon.

Pages 98, 118, 135, 145, 214: © Jean Claude Golvin, Watercolours from L'Égypte restituée, Éditions Errance, Paris.

Page 119: © Leslie Greener / National Geographic Society.

Pages 86, 156 middle: Jürgen Liepe, Berlin.

We extend our special thanks to Alberto Berengo Gardin for preparing the plans on pages 11, 29, 32, 34, 36, 39, 41, 48, 50, 51, 56, 61, 70, 78, 98, 102, 114, 122, 123, 130, 132, 139, 140, 152, 155, 160, 178/179, 181, 184, 185, 195, 198, 205, 218.

ALL 40 TITLES AT A GLANCE

Each book: US$ 29.99 | £ 16.99 | CDN$ 39.95

The Ancient World
- ▶ The Near East
- ▶ Egypt
- ▶ Greece
- ▶ The Roman Empire
- ▶ The Greco-Roman Orient

The Medieval World
- ▶ Byzantium
- ▶ The Early Middle Ages
- ▶ The Romanesque
- ▶ High Gothic
- ▶ Late Gothic

The pre-Colombian World
- ▶ The Maya
- ▶ Mexico
- ▶ The Aztecs
- ▶ Peru
- ▶ The Incas

Islamic Masterpieces
- ▶ Islam from Baghdad to Cordoba
- ▶ Islam from Cairo to Granada
- ▶ Persia
- ▶ Turkey
- ▶ Mogul

The Splendours of Asia
- ▶ Hindu India
- ▶ Buddhist India
- ▶ China
- ▶ South-East Asia
- ▶ Japan

Stylistic Developments from 1400
- ▶ Renaissance
- ▶ Baroque in Italy
- ▶ Baroque in Central Europe
- ▶ Hispanic Baroque
- ▶ French Classicism

The Modern Age
- ▶ Neo-Classicism and Revolution
- ▶ American Architecture
- ▶ Art Nouveau
- ▶ Early Modern Architecture
- ▶ Visionary Masters
- ▶ Monumental Modern
- ▶ International Style
- ▶ Post-Modernism
- ▶ New Forms
- ▶ Contemporary Masters

"... a truly remarkable publishing event in architecture."
The Architectural Review
London

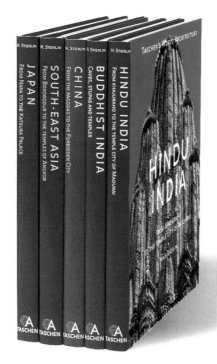

- ▶ Collect 40 volumes of TASCHEN'S WORLD ARCHITECTURE in eight years (1996–2003) and build up a complete panorama of world architecture from the earliest buildings of Mesopotamia to the latest contemporary projects.

- ▶ The series is grouped into five-volume units, each devoted to the architectural development of a major civilisation, and introducing the reader to many new and unfamiliar worlds.

- ▶ Each volume covers a complex architectural era and is written so vividly that most readers will feel the urge to go out and discover these magnificent buildings for themselves.

TASCHEN'S WORLD ARCHITECTURE

"An excellently produced, informative guide to the history of architecture. Accessible to everyone."

Architektur Aktuell, Vienna

"This is by far the most comprehensive review of recent years."

Frankfurter Rundschau, Frankfurt

"A successful debut of a very promising series."

Architektur & Wohnen, Hamburg, on *Islam from Baghdad to Cordoba*

"…each theme is presented in a very interesting, lively style… it makes you want to set off straight away to see everything with your own eyes."

Baumeister, Munich, on *The Roman Empire*

▶ TASCHEN'S WORLD ARCHITECTURE presents 6000 years of architectural history in 40 volumes.

▶ Each volume is a detailed and authoritative study of one specific era.

▶ The whole series provides a comprehensive survey of architecture from antiquity to the present day. Five volumes will be published each year.

▶ TASCHEN'S WORLD ARCHITECTURE is a must for all lovers of architecture and travel.

▶ Renowned photographers have travelled the world for this series, presenting more than 12000 photographs of famous and lesser-known buildings.

▶ Expert authors guide the reader through TASCHEN'S WORLD ARCHITECTURE with exciting, scientifically well-founded texts that place architecture within the cultural, political and social context of each era.

▶ The elegant, modern design and the clear, visually striking layout guide the reader through the historical and contemporary world of architecture.

▶ Influential architectural theories, typical stylistic features and specific construction techniques are separately explained on eye-catching pages.

▶ Each volume includes between 40 and 50 maps, plans and structural drawings based on the latest scholarly findings and are produced for this series using state-of-the-art computer technology.

▶ The appendix contains clear chronological tables, giving an instant overview of the correlation between the historical events and architecture of any given civilisation.

▶ A detailed glossary clearly explains architectural terms.

▶ An index of names and places ensures quick and easy reference to specific buildings and people.

▶ Each book contains 240 pages with some 300 color illustrations on high-quality art paper. 240 x 300 mm, hardcover with dust jacket.

Each book: US$ 29.99 | £ 16.99 | CDN$ 39.95